Samuel Wilberforce

Personal responsibility of man

sermons preached during the season of Lent, 1868, in Oxford

Samuel Wilberforce

Personal responsibility of man
sermons preached during the season of Lent, 1868, in Oxford

ISBN/EAN: 9783744745000

Printed in Europe, USA, Canada, Australia, Japan

Cover: Foto ©Lupo / pixelio.de

More available books at **www.hansebooks.com**

Personal Responsibility of Man.

SERMONS

PREACHED DURING

THE SEASON OF LENT, 1868,

IN

OXFORD.

BY

THE LORD BISHOP OF OXFORD.   THE LORD ABP. OF YORK.
THE DEAN OF ELY.   E. B. PUSEY, D.D.
H. L. MANSEL, D.D.   A. POTT, B.D.
H. W. BURROWS, B.D.   T. T. CARTER, M.A.
R. SCOTT, D.D.

WITH A PREFACE

BY

SAMUEL, LORD BISHOP OF OXFORD.

Oxford,

AND 377, STRAND, LONDON:

JAMES PARKER AND CO.

1869.

PREFACE.

———◆———

THE subject of these Sermons seemed to us
to follow in a natural sequence that of the
former year.   It is undoubtedly one of the deepest moment : one, too, well qualified to arouse
in every soul a sense of the awfulness of possessing such gifts as God has bestowed upon us and
not using them to His glory.   May He of His
mercy speak this lesson home to our souls.

S. OXON.

CONTENTS.

———◆———

SERMON I.

As the Creature of God.

ROMANS xi. 36.

"For of Him, and through Him, and to Him, are all things:
to whom be glory for ever. Amen."

THIS is, indeed, one of the grandest utterances of
this wonderful Epistle. We can almost see the
acting of the Apostle's soul as its mighty waves raise
themselves up under the breath of the awful Spirit
which sweeps over them. He has been gazing on the
footsteps of God's wonderful providence across the
wastes of time. The long Gentile estrangedness, the
Jewish adoption, and the Jewish fall; the faithfulness
of God amidst the manifold workings of man's unfaithfulness; the love, the might, and the marvel of
His counsels, all these pass in review before him, until
the struggling thoughts burst forth into adoration, " O
the depth of the riches both of the wisdom and knowledge of God ! how unsearchable are His judgments,
and His ways past finding out ! For who hath known
the mind of the Lord ? or who hath been His coun-
sellor?" And then from the marvel of these hidden
counsels the Apostle's thoughts turn to the mystery of
His sovereignty. "Who hath first given unto Him?"
Until all is summed up in these words of wonder:
" For of Him, and through Him, and to Him, are all
things : to whom be glory for ever."

It is on the consequence which flows directly from the truth involved in this ascription that I am now to speak to you,—the personal responsibility of each one of you to God as your Creator. Brethren, join, I beseech you, with me in one earnest cry to the Eternal Spirit, that He would awaken this night in many a heart the sense of this, which, as we muse upon it, we shall, I think, see to be the one all-controlling law of our being.

Now to lead your thoughts to dwell upon this great subject with something like an orderly progression, I would ask you to enter with me into these considerations.

I. What He is of whom we speak.

II. What we are.

III. Why we are what He has so made us to be.

IV. The consequences which flow, first, as regards Him ; and, secondly, as regards ourselves from this relation between Him and us.

I. What, then, is He of whom we speak.

He is the One eternal necessary Self-existing, All-wise, All-mighty, All-loving, Being, from whom all things are that are ; who of His mere will made them to be ; who upholds them in being by His mere will· He is *ONE*, not one as we are amongst many, but *ONE* absolutely. THE UNITY ; One in Himself ; the Principle of oneness, of whom, through whom, to whom, are all things. And this He ever has been, and ever must be. There was no beginning to this being, there is no prolongation of it, there is no ending to it. It is One, simply One. "From everlasting to everlasting Thou art God." Till we can grasp something of this idea we cannot really understand in its first conditions the relations of the creature and the Creator. For to do this, we must see that He was the same when no created being was, that He would be still the same if there were no creation ; that He was as blessed, as perfect, as glorious in Himself, when self-contained in the solitude of the eternal rest ere creation was, as when it had pleased Him to people the heavens and the earth with reasonable life derived from Himself. We must understand that He is essentially external to His creation, though it owes to Him its first and its continued being. As WE may look through the microscope and see in a drop of water its living denizens, but are ourselves external to that drop of water, so is God Himself, in His own essence, external to His universe. It is for Him, from Him ; but He is not in it ; He is not in time, or in space ; He is not extended, or diffused through time, or through space ; He is all-present everywhere. And all is that is, because He wills that it should be ; and it is for His glory which is and must be that for which, all that is, is. This, then, is our Creator.

II. Next, what are we ? Creatures whom He has made to be. Whom, further, He has made to be so far as the creature can be, in His image after His likeness ; to whom He has given the awful dower of personality, whom He has gathered severally up into a unity of being, which is in its measure the image of His unity, so that each one of us stands in the midst of the multitude of beings round us alone ; no other of those like us able to intrude into the essential singleness of our own separate being. Further, He has bound up this mystery of our unity by the band of a will, making us hereby real units not only as regards others, but even as regards Himself. Further, that He has made us capable of knowing, communing with and loving Him, and therefore under the action of our will capable of either rendering real service to Him, of returning real love to Him, or of really rebelling against Him. Yet, further, He has set us in a state of progression, has planted in us abundantly the seeds of an unlimited development, with power of increase which, so far as we can see, are unbounded, and which He has promised, if we seek Him, to develope for us and in us beyond what eye hath seen, or ear heard, or than it has entered into the heart of man to conceive. And yet, once more, to give room for this development He has made us whom He has thus called out of nothing into being, partakers of His own never-ending condition ; so that once being, we must be for ever. Time for us runs not out into nothingness, but into eternity ; an eternity which we may spend in His presence and blessedness, or in perpetual banishment from Him.

This, then, is what we are; and, III. See why He has made us so to be.

From the essential love which He is. He made us not of caprice, not to exert His own power, but of love, for God is love. He needed not any. No created being could add anything to the calm, perfect, necessary blessedness of the eternal self-sufficing Godhead. But His love was prolific, and poured out itself into a reasonable creation, whose blessedness should be His glory. This, then, is, I. What He is ; II. What we are ; III. Why we are what He has made us.

And now, mark IV. some of the consequences which must flow from this relation of Him to us, and of us to Him. And first, the consequence as to Him. Surely it is plainly this, that His right over us is absolute and unlimited. He is the Lord our God. What can the thing formed say to Him who with power, and love,

and wisdom infinite has formed it? If, then, this be
the consequence as to Him, the first consequence to
us must be that which is the correlative of this absolute right in Him, namely, an absolute submission.
We are His. Bear for a moment the thought. Thou
art at all, only because God's love and power made
thee to be. Go back up the stream of time but a
few years, and where wast thou, and what wast thou?
nowhere and nothing. The least and most inconsider-
able thing that then was, was greater by all the vast
immeasurable interval which parts being from nothingness than thou. The smallest insect that floated on
the evening air was of more worth than thou, for it
was, and thou wast not. And out of that nothingness
He called thee into being to be blessed in serving
Him. The first consequence of which as regards thee
must be that thou art His absolutely; the creature of
His hand. And next follows this consequence, that as
He made thee of His love to serve Him, and be like
Him, only in so serving Him canst thou be happy.
For He cannot change, and thou, though thou canst by
a free will misused, pervert and render crooked thy
being, canst not alter the law on which He planned its
lines. Thou the creature canst in the mystery of thy
true separate being mar His work, but thou canst not
give it another perfectness than that which He designed it for. From both of which consequences follows another, namely, that thy being, in its truest and
most essential existence, is really spent with Him alone
in time and in eternity. This is the necessary consequence of that mystery of personality which He has
imparted from Himself to us. It is true that in one
sense we are in the midst of a crowd, but in a far
deeper and truer sense we are still alone with Him.

We have others like ourselves around us, near us, and yet we are alone.   They touch us, and yet we are untouched.   In the greatest and deepest things we are severed from every other.   We struggle against the mysterious law of singleness only to find ourselves utterly baffled by its close, clinging, irresistible power.   We long to impart ourselves to another, and we cannot ; the invisible wall of personality parts us from them.   We touch, like globes, at a point, we cannot commingle our beings.   Yes, in the thickest crowd *WE* the true we, are alone.   We can see this law acting on others, from birth to death.   Look at a little child sleeping, and stirring in its sleep.   How alone it is,—there in that small cradle is all the volume of a spirit which shall pervade eternity.   You gaze, but you cannot commune, you cannot track the actings of that spirit. And as to all the deepest beings of the soul, the mystery only increases as life goes on, and some small measures of intercommunion of spirit become ours.   For as to all the hidden mysteries of our souls, no one knows us, we know no one, and yet ONE is ever with us who knows all, who sees us through and through, whose presence wraps us round so close, that sleeping or waking, we never in our inmost being escape for one moment from His gaze, and His touch, to whom we know we can impart our whole selves, from whom we feel that we can never escape, to whom even in spite of ourselves our spirit will cry out, " Thou hast beset me behind and before, and laid Thy hand upon me ᵃ." With whom, then, are we indeed living ?   Surely not with these shadows round us, which in spite of all our efforts have at best so impalpable a presence as to us, but with Him in whom we live and move, and have our

---

ᵃ Ps. cxxxix. 5.

being. Solus cum solo ; this is the awful sentence of our
consciousness.   Nor is it only in our consciousness that
this law of singleness acts; all our being is held under
it ; every voluntary acting of the life He has given us,
not outward actions only, but the most inward conscious stirrings of the mind and spirit, each thought,
each desire, which can touch no other, reach straight
to Him ; in all these things no other can share with us
the obligations which living, in its every waking moment, imposes on us, and no one therefore can share
in the discharge of them, or in their consequences.
They exist between the creature and the Creator alone,
they are the correlative of single, personal, reasonable,
creaturely being, incommunicable, inevitable ; no one
can be bound for us, no one can act for us, no one can
suffer for us.   It is a true, real, personal responsibility ;
it clings to us, it never leaves us.   Every allowed thought,
desire, imagination ; every word spoken, every act done
consciously, is either a fulfilment, or a break of the ever
acting law of our creaturely existence.   From the lightest
stirrings of that being in which consciousness scarcely
acts, up to those in which there is a mighty concentra-
tion of passion or will, every one is the acting of the
personal unit of separated life according to the mystery of its will against or for its supreme ruler and its
own perfectness.   And, further, all this is ever going on
under His eye.   The closest to us know little of it.
Life in its essential actings is such a secret thing.   Thick
curtains cover the deep mystery of being.   They shut
in such volumes of existence, whilst they shut out well-
nigh all the pryings of the most curious gazers.   But
all is ever naked and open unto Him.   All those secret
stirrings of life, each motive in its varying force and
colour, the measure of every effort, the true amount

of every resistance, all the finest shadings on which the
moral impulse depends for its defining character, all
are most exactly seen by Him. On all, His judgment is ever passing, yea, and in all the incidents of
that inward conflict He is, (until His Spirit has been
grieved utterly,) Himself taking a part. Over those
first highest fountains of life His Spirit broods. The
chaos, all unconscious of the Presence, is surging in its
blind contentions under a controlling, vivifying power ;
there in the recesses of personal being is the supreme
Lord striving with and for His creature.

Surely such a life as this is in very deed spent with
Him alone, under a close clinging law of most real
personal responsibility. And if this be true of our life
in time, how far more true must it be of our life in
eternity. For here, in very compassion to our weakness, His Presence is often veiled from us. Trees of the
garden soften for us what, unsheltered, would be its too
excessive brightness. Forms of others, shadowy as
they are, thronging around us, conceal from us our
otherwise too intolerable loneliness. But these miti-
gating accidents of our life here cannot be with us
there, where all who enter see as they are seen, and
know as they are known. There every soul must feel
for ever either to its woe unutterable or to its bliss infinite, that "of Him, and through Him, and to Him are
all things." There the loneliness of him who has not
learned to know all things in God must be infinite and
eternal. There all the life which each one has led here
will be open and plain before Him, sharp and clear,
veiled by no disguises, softened by no excuses. There
each rebel will see, as though it were written with a sun-
beam, that he received his being from God to spend it
for His glory, and in this light of truth escape will be

impossible from the overwhelming sense of the personal responsibility of every soul to the God who called it into being.

Brethren, if all this be true, surely it is a truth which must swallow up everything beside. All lesser and accidental conditions vanish in the sight of this tremendous reality. The life which looks the poorest and the meanest is lifted up immeasurably, if only it be a due fulfilling of this law of personal responsibility. For every act so done, though in the smallest earthly circle, is the sowing of the life with seeds of eternal endurance. Such a life is a true loyal acceptance of its own personal responsibility to God, and so a yielding it to Him, and therefore a being moulded by Him, a growing fit for a blessedness in His presence, so supreme and entrancing that our poor conceptions here cannot reach even to define its conditions.

And, on the other hand, the life which looks the grandest here, which, it may be, is the noblest in the triumphs of intellect or power, may yet be nothing else than one prolonged rebellion. For notice, that such a life is nothing else than a perpetually augmenting catalogue of sins. Acts which in themselves, taken as mere acts, may have no distinct colour of evil, yet become expressions of the highest evil, if they are wrought as separate resistances of the will of the creature to the will of God. Look in this light at the growth of an ordinary life which, within the Church of Christ, refuses to yield itself to the will of God, and carries out that refusal to its furthest limits. In the earliest stage, there is the self-pleasing of childhood; but if the child is naturally affectionate, sweet-tempered, or high-spirited, there may be nothing to catch attention in that child's life but what is beautiful and

attractive. Yet even at this age the evil may have
begun. There may be a turning away of that young
heart from the secret drawings of the blessed Spirit,
which is beginning to substitute fatally the rule of self-
will for that of obedience to the will of God. And
the next stage of life shews the evil advancing : a love
of display or the rule of sense begins to shew itself;
as yet, perhaps, in no offensive or repulsive outbreaks,
but so that the keen eye even of earthly love may
trace its presence. Then comes the time when sensual
appetite in the one sex and the passion for admiration
in the other clamour for indulgence, and when opportunity of gratifying such demands is seldom lacking.
And now the blight upon the highest actings of the
soul is visible even outwardly. The one character becomes frivolous, vain, and heartless ; the other becomes
the prey of a gross sensuality which tyrannises over all
its nobler impulses. The common poison root of
a violated personal responsibility is casting its evil fibres
round every natural shoot of spiritual, moral, and even
intellectual excellence. Every acting of the curiously
composite life is disordered : the sense of truth, the
power of sustained exertion, the nobleness of self-sacri-
fice, the patience of an enduring struggle, all are becoming impossible ; whilst to the palled appetite fiercer
excitement becomes needful to obtain the gross pleasures for which the soul is bartering its all. Dissipation in its wildness, gambling in its madness, de-
bauchery in its foulness ; these are the after stages,
and when these have been passed through there break
forth every now and then monstrous and unnatural
forms of wickedness as though to attest the presence
of that principle of rebellion which is in all its fulness possessing the soul ; or if these do not appear,

then those darker powers of our nature which are meant to form the deep background of the whole moral being act diseasedly through wrong channels and with disordered violence. Gall and bitterness pervade the character. The pleasant and often attractive sins of youth grow into the repulsive forms of jealousy, envy, hatred, and maliciousness. And this change cannot pass upon the moral nature without a corresponding evil visiting the spiritual. Neglect of God grows through often repeated acts of conscious resistance into wilful rebellion, first against His law, then against His nature, and at last against His being. Alas, the fatal stages may be too surely traced, as one by one they are passed through by falling souls. They are such as these: conscience dishonoured, doubts first allowed and then encouraged, the whisper of unbelief first barely listened to and then communed with as a pleasant voice. Then come scoffings and blasphemies, atheism and destruction.

Here is the history of such a course, where all its parts are acted openly and completely out. But this differs only in degree from the history of every self-willed life. Weaker passions, less opportunity of indulging them, outward restraints, a softer fibre of the moral nature, above all, the cloaking presence of a necessary respectability, hide the process from our eyes. But it is there. Every thoroughly self-willed soul must under the law of personal responsibility have made itself a hater of its God.

In one respect there is a peculiar awfulness in these commoner, and, as they seem, lighter instances of evil, for in them the poison, though it works so thoroughly, works so secretly. They may therefore be fearfully common; and as the last aggravation of their terror

they may be unsuspected not only by others but even
by their unconscious victim. The restraint of circumstance, his own decency, his fatal respectability, these
hide from him his true condition, until life is spent, until
the day of grace is closed, until the possibility of an
amendment is gone, until the will in the mystery of its
acting under or against grace is irrecoverably hardened.
What an awakening must death be from such a life !
When the breath of God sweeps away suddenly all the
mists which have hindered the soul from seeing its true
state ; when it wakes up alone with God ; when it sees
His holiness, and is perfectly conscious of its hatred to
that holiness and to Him the Holy One ; when it knows
within itself that for it under love infinite rejected, and
Almighty grace resisted, the mystery of personal being
has been brought out so as even of necessity to end in
everlasting death.

The sight is horrible, yet let us look at it long
enough to have its lineaments so fixed in our memory
that they may stand between us and our evil desires
in the hour of strong temptation. For such need not
to be the state of any one of us. Christ has redeemed us from all evil. The powers of the Eternal
Spirit are with us, the long-suffering love of God yearns
over us. In us the good purpose of God in bestowing on us the awful gift of personal being may yet,
through His grace, be accomplished in our everlasting
blessedness. Only fight against the beginnings of rebelliousness ; only pray earnestly against your temptations to it ; only keep God's watch against those
accesses of appetite and passion by which, as by the
sweetness of baits, the great rebel draws you to his side,
and all shall be well. Use meditation ; daily if possible,
and if that be not possible, as frequent as you may, to

withdraw you from outer things into that presence in
which all temptations fade away, all things assume their
true proportions; in which is quietness for the spirit of
man; in which, as in the dewy freshness of the morning, all graces grow; in which love to God is shed
abroad in the heart, and from which you go forth
another man to the struggle and strife of your daily
warfare with evil.

Beware, too, of allowing any sense of distance to
grow up between God and your soul.   Any indulged
sin of heart, of desire, of thought, or of act, tends at
once to create it.   Then indolence pleads that by degrees that sense of distance will of itself, without your
troubling yourself about it, die away, and that you will
be where you were of old.   But it is not so.   That passing sense of distance soon hardens itself into a habit
if it be not at once removed.   Whenever, therefore,
you are conscious of it search earnestly to find its
cause.   Cast the lot of God until you have found the
hidden wedge of gold and the goodly Babylonish gar-
ment, and bring them forth and burn them before the
Lord, lest that lot be cast against thee, and take thee
to thy destruction.   Use faithfully the blessed mediation of the Eternal Son.   Rest your soul on His sacrifice once offered for you on the cross.   Doubt not for
an instant that there is full, free, sure pardon for every
one who turns from his sin to God; that we "have an
Advocate with the Father, Jesus Christ the righteous."
Trust to that mediation.   Do it honour.   Return through
it at once to thy Father.   In any allowed estrangedness
from Him is the seed of rebellion and of ruin.   And
then revenge upon yourself your provocations of Him.
Do not pass them by; He blesses such discipline of
yourself, and under that blessing it breeds in your soul
tenderness, watchfulness, and love to Him.

It will aid you, too, in practising the yielding of the will to Him, and in this is the master secret of all spiritual growth. This, in sorrow, plucks the sharpest sting out of the anguish ; this sweetens the asperity and the ruggedness of a temper naturally uneven ; this sanctifies the affections. As the voice of the heart becomes indeed "not my will but Thine be done," the work is accomplished, the moral discipline has been perfected, the spiritual renewal under the hand of God the Holy Ghost has been wrought. The golden stairs lie straight before you, and turning on their adamantine hinges the golden gates which lead into the city shall open for you of their own accord.

Thither, by the might of His Holy Spirit, through the atonement wrought for us by the Incarnate Son, may the Eternal Father bring at last every one of us His ransomed and regenerate creatures.

Now to God the Father, the Son, and the Holy Ghost, be might, majesty, and dominion, for ever and ever. Amen.

SERMON II.

Personal Responsibility of Man, as entrusted with a Revelation.

GALATIANS i. 15, 16.

"But when it pleased God, who separated me from my mother's womb, and called me by His grace, to reveal His Son in me, that I might preach Him among the heathen; immediately I conferred not with flesh and blood."

M Y subject this evening, Christian brethren, is "the Personal Responsibility of Man, as entrusted with a Revelation :" and I have thought it well to introduce it to you, not by any abstract discussion of the nature and limits and results of that responsibility, but by the exhibition of a notable case—perhaps *the* most notable case in history—in which a revelation was definitely made and the consequent responsibility consciously and avowedly accepted, and followed out to its legitimate consequences.

St. Paul speaks in the text of God having been pleased to reveal His Son *in him*, that is, in St. Paul; and it is necessary at once to observe that the meaning which the merely English reader of this Scripture would probably attach to the words is not exactly its true meaning. "To reveal His Son *in* me," might seem to imply some internal revelation, some process within the Apostle's own heart and moral being, which gave him an absolute and infallible knowledge of the truth of Christ. I do not say that there was nothing at all of this kind, I think there was: it seems incapable of contradiction, that whenever the heart of a man is truly converted to God the work must be, and always is, the work of the Holy Spirit, and cannot be merely the result of thinking, or reasoning, or arguing: and therefore, although it is perfectly true that such a view of the conversion of the human heart is capable of being abused and distorted into fanatical errors, still the view itself must be prized and maintained. That, however, to which St. Paul more immediately referred was a different thing: when he said "God hath revealed His Son *in* me," he intended rather to refer to the fact that God intended to reveal His Son to mankind *by* and *through* him; he was to be the instrument of the revelation: he was "a chosen vessel to preach the Gospel." God had revealed Christ to *him*, that *he* might reveal Him to others; and so the meaning is, not so much that a light was lighted by divine power *in* the mind of St. Paul, as that a light was intended to shine out *from* him for the illumination of the world.

So that, after all, perhaps the difference between the two interpretations is not so wide as it seems. It may be a great matter to the critic to determine whether the particle, which St. Paul used, be translated to mean 'within,' or to mean 'by' or 'through:' but really when weighed in spiritual scales the two meanings come much to the same thing, or at all events one implies the other; for God can never make a revelation of His Son *through* a man, until He has first made the revelation *within* him: the lamp cannot illuminate until the light has been lighted within it: the light shines *without*, because it shines *within;* and if St. Paul could speak confidently of God having been pleased to call him by His grace, and to reveal Christ through him to

the heathen, it was because he could speak confidently
of that revelation of Christ to his own soul, which had
so thoroughly converted his mind and changed the purpose of his life. For how stood the fact? Saul, as we
all know, was going to Damascus to persecute the
Christians; on the way Jesus Christ spoke to him:
in a certain sense it was not the first time that Christ
had spoken to him: he must have heard a good deal
about Christ, and have formed a very strong opinion
concerning Him; he must have seen with that penetrating intellect which so strikingly marked him, that
either the faith of Christ or the traditions of his fathers
must perish; but he had never for a moment realized
who and what Jesus Christ was: that knowledge came
to him when he was struck down to the earth, and the
exceeding bright light from heaven shined upon him.
I cannot say exactly how the knowledge came to him
even then; as the Egyptian magicians said, "It was
the finger of God;" but Jesus Christ *spoke* to him,—we
know *that:* the utterance was apparently simple, "Saul,
Saul, why persecutest thou *Me?*" but it was an utterance that was "quick and powerful, and sharper than
any two-edged sword," because it was "the Word of
God;" and no sooner had that revelation of Jesus Christ
penetrated into Saul's heart, supported and strengthened
as it was by further and fuller revelations, than the per-
secutor became a preacher, and the enemy of Christ
became His Apostle, and old things passed away and
all things became new; there was a new purpose, and
a new object of love, and a new work, and new hopes:
in the language most appropriate to the subject of this
sermon, St. Paul felt his responsibility as being "entrusted with a revelation." And so it was that he was
in the habit of expressing himself very strongly con-

cerning this responsibility. He said that "necessity
was laid upon him," that he had a Gospel to preach,
and that preach it he must; it was no question of
choice, but of absolute and inevitable constraint. No
doubt he had felt responsibility before; every earnest
man does; no man can be fit for a post of trust,
whether high or low, whether as a servant or as a
prince, who does not feel responsibility; but the responsibility felt by a man conscious, as St. Paul was,
that Christ has spoken to him, is deeper and more
energetic than all other responsibilities, as heaven is
higher than earth and God greater than man. God
speaks, man *must* obey. So thought and felt St. Paul;
and, humanly speaking, the history of the Church, and
the present condition of Christendom, and the religious
life of your souls, Christian brethren, are to a great extent the result of the fact, that St. Paul felt his responsibility as a man, *in* and *through* whom God had been
pleased to reveal His blessed Son.

Let us leave St. Paul, however, for a few moments,
and let me remind you how that God has from the
beginning revealed Himself to man, and that the spiritual condition of man before God has depended upon
the way in which he has received the revelation. To
be able to receive a revelation from God, this is one
mark of humanity; and to be able to reject the revelation, this is another. In a certain sense, a very sad
and painful sense I admit, but still a certain sense, the
power of rejecting a revelation is even more distinctive
of humanity than the power of receiving it. What I
mean is this: God takes the clay, and, like the potter,
forms such vessels as He will, and He puts into those
vessels what He pleases; and when He made all things
at the beginning, He impressed His own will upon

them, and declared them to be "very good;" and really
the first thing that made an unspeakable gulph between man and the other creatures which God had
created was the act of disobedience, that is, the rejec-
tion of God's revelation.   Put yourself in the first man's
position.   God reveals Himself by a command: "Eat
not of the forbidden tree; in the day that thou eatest
thou shalt die."   That was Adam's *Bible*, it was emphatically the *Old* Testament, the first and earliest
covenant between God and man; and Adam did not
feel his responsibility as a being entrusted with a
revelation; it did not rule his life and control his
actions; he did not consider what mighty issues depended upon his mode of dealing with his trust.   Yea,
hath God said this?   *You* not to touch a tree which
is so pleasant to the eye, so good for food, and so
much to be desired to make one wise?   *You* not to use
your reason?   *You* to be tied down by paltry, arbi-
trary, unmeaning rules? and so forth.   Oh! there was
rationalism in Paradise, and it was Satan that intro-
duced it; and because man allowed Satan to lead him
astray, and would not simply bend himself to the revealed truth of God, therefore he fell into sin.

Next observe that the whole course of sacred history,
since the days of Adam, has been a history of revelations.   God has *revealed, unveiled, discovered* Himself
to this man and to that, in order that he to whom God
has been revealed may reveal Him to others; the process of which St. Paul speaks when he says, "to reveal
His Son *in* me," is the very process which has been
going on from the beginning.   Look at Noah.   God revealed Himself to Noah at a time of great darkness and
wickedness; and when the Apostle, in the Epistle to
the Hebrews, speaks of Noah in his grand catalogue of

men of faith, as of one who being warned by God of
things not seen as yet was moved with fear and built
an ark to the saving of his house, he means to say that
he was a man who felt his responsibility as entrusted
with a revelation from God ; that revelation of wrath to
come was a trust ; how should it be dealt with ? Should
it be despised ? should it be reasoned about ? should it
be ridiculed ? should Noah's ingenuity be employed to
prove that it could not be true ?   No : God had spoken,
and therefore all such conduct would be wicked and
absurd ; there was but one way of dealing with such
a trust ; " according to all that God commanded, so did
he." Well done, Noah ! That is faith shewing itself in
works; that is the true way of shewing a sense of responsibility.

Look at Abraham.   " The Lord had *said* unto Abraham." That is the very beginning of his history. The
world had got into a very bad state, there was very
little knowledge of God, very little fear of Him, I
should suppose not much love of Him; and when it
pleased God to commence that series of revelations
which culminated in Jesus Christ His Son, He did it by
speaking to one chosen minister ; He revealed Himself
in Abraham, and He told Abraham that he must leave
his country and his father's house, and go into a strange
land, and there become a great people, and the source
of blessing to the whole world. What did Abraham do ?
He simply obeyed.   I suppose it cost him as great an
effort to leave his home and emigrate to a strange country as it would have cost one of us.   But he did it : he
felt under constraint, not his own master ; the word
which God had spoken to him,—however it was spoken,
and this I do not know,—this word became his law ; the
responsibility of having received a revelation ruled all

his subsequent conduct; he, like Noah, and unlike Adam and Eve, did not reason about the matter, and try to evade the commands of God, but he simply submitted himself to those commands, even when they would seem to rob him of his chief treasure, and sacrifice his only son.   And so Abraham, like Noah, and unlike Adam and Eve, gained a place in that Apostolic roll of men of faith to which I referred before. " He went out," says the Apostle, "not knowing whither he went:" no, but he knew *why;* and he who knows the *why*, and can find ,the answer in the revelation of God, need not trouble himself about the *whither*.

Once more, look at Moses. You see precisely the same characteristics of conduct. He, too, received a revelation from God ; and the pressure of the responsibility which that revelation brought with it is made all the more conspicuous by the fact that Moses shrank from it, and tried to evade it. His shy, gentle, retiring spirit saw nothing tempting in the leadership of a nation, and much that was very repulsive in being set up in opposition to Pharaoh : and I believe that many notable men who have figured in the world's history have been in like manner meek, retiring men, who have been forced into action by the overwhelming sense of duty ; certainly no instance can be more striking than that of Moses. The vision of the burning bush, the proclamation of the Name of God, the clear announcement of the mission to Israel, all these pressed upon Moses' conscience. Still he would escape if he could. Might not Aaron go ? Were there not many men more suitable for the work—bolder, stronger, better, than he ? No, there must be no excuse, and Moses dares not be disobedient. The responsibility of having received a revelation from

God triumphs over everything, and so Moses became
what he was.

And what was he ? why, another and one of the chief
of those men of faith who " subdued kingdoms, wrought
righteousness, obtained promises." And let me say in
general that men of faith and men who feel their responsibility, as having received a revelation from God,
are men of the same class, or rather the same men
described in different ways. Faith implies a revelation,
and men of faith are just those who feel that a revelation must not be trifled with, must not be set aside,
must not be contemned, but must be adopted as the
law of life. Let me strengthen this view by reminding
you that the catalogue in the eleventh chapter of Hebrews, to which I have been referring, is remarkable for
the absence of two names : it does not contain the name
of Adam, and it does not contain the name of Jesus
Christ : and why not ? For very different reasons. Not the
first Adam, for, alas ! he despised God's revelation ; not
the second, for He was the revelation Himself. Christ
our Lord was not a man of faith, because He was one
with the Father ; and it would be an insult to Him to
speak of His responsibility as having received a revelation from God, because He alone saw the Father unveiled from all eternity, and came down from heaven in
infinite condescension to reveal Him to mankind. Oh !
it is a melancholy thing to think upon, that the list of
men conspicuous for their faith should want the name
of him who is the father of us all, who was created in
the image of God, and to whom first God made a revelation of Himself ; but it is not melancholy to miss from
the list the name of the second Adam, because the
omission marks Him out as the Lord from heaven, and

because likewise His perfect obedience to the will of
God, without strain, without effort, without any apparent
pressure of a sense of responsibility, may teach us that
our own sense of responsibility should be manifested,
not by strife or debate, but by simple submission to
God's will.

But now, Christian brethren, let us look a little more
closely at our own position with respect to this matter.
We wish to regard ourselves as laid under a pressure of
responsibility by the fact of our having received a revelation from God. And certainly it is impossible to deny
that responsibility, without denying everything that
makes us men ; even those who would make the least
of the revelation of God in Jesus Christ, and of the
peculiar position in which we stand as Christians, would
still, I apprehend, maintain that God had revealed Himself to us in some manner, and that the revelation had
certain moral consequences. But the point for which we
have to contend, the thing which we really mean, and
which unfortunately many people will deny, is this, that
we have received from God a definite revelation which
can be expressed in words, and which is contained in
God's own Book. We have to maintain that this volume
contains a divine account of the divers manners in which
God has made Himself known to our fathers, and
notably of that transcendent revelation which He has
made to us in the person of His own Son. We are not
bound to tie ourselves down to any special theory concerning the composition of the book, the machinery (so
to speak) of its construction, the manner in which God's
Spirit has been breathed into it ; but we *are* bound to
hold that it contains God's revelation of Himself, and
that in it and through it we are to seek humbly, as
members of the Church to whose keeping the book

has been entrusted, for the knowledge of His will. I
am not going to enter upon an elaborate discussion of
a very difficult subject, but I wish to observe that to my
own mind the objections so often and so flippantly made
to what is called a *book-revelation*, are, both upon religious and philosophical grounds, frivolous and empty.
The religious ground need hardly be argued ; because
if we have no *book-revelation*, if the Holy Scriptures be
not the revelation of God, it is impossible to say that
any religion exists at all, except that dim feeling after
God which we call natural religion, and which has
proved during many sad centuries of human history,
and is proving in some parts of the world still, its utter
impotence to do more than erect an altar, as it did at
Athens, to the " Unknown God." But I would have you
to perceive that, giving up for the moment the religious
ground, it is not reasonable or philosophical to make light
of a book-revelation, or to deny its possibility. For what
is a book, but imprinted language? And what is language,
but the very mark of man's supremacy, the very electric
current which enables the influence of heaven to enter
his soul? What is it but thought, the outcoming of
mind, of the truly human faculties, and so the indica-
tion that man has been created worthy of a revelation
from heaven, and that he is likely to receive one? I
can conceive other ways by which God may and does
to a certain extent make Himself known to man. I do
not wish to depreciate any one of these ways. He
speaks in nature, He speaks by providence, He speaks
by the conscience, which tells man of good and evil,
and by those inward questionings which lead us to
guess whence we have come and whither we are going ;
but surely no one of these means of communication is
so wonderful or so effective as that of human speech,

that transformation of matter into thought, that change by which "the very dross of the body is used for the coinage of the mind*." And therefore when I find it solemnly asserted that God, having first created man in His own image, afterwards assumed that image in very deed Himself, and that in human flesh and blood He spoke to us concerning Himself, and when I find a record of this great visit of Him who made Himself known as the *Word*, and I find moreover that this record has proved (as I might have expected that it would) to be the source of a new spiritual life in the world, and that all that is most bright and hopeful is connected with it,—why am I to say that it cannot be the revelation of God? what homage do I do to philosophy or reason by rejecting that, which comes to me as the Holy Scriptures have come, and which is commended to me as they are commended?

Of course it is impossible for me to enter fully into an argument which has already filled libraries; but I think it right to warn you in passing against the flippant tone of lofty condescension, with which persons often speak of the Holy Scriptures. I say that although it is very easy to make a flippant remark or a damaging observation, yet the whole argument for the truth of Holy Scripture as the revelation of God, is a massive argument, which cannot be successfully assailed; and though efforts have been made in all generations to sap its foundations, those foundations are too deep to be sapped, and go down to the solid rock of the truth of the eternal God.

My business, however, is not so much to prove to you

* For this striking view of human speech I am indebted to a lecture "On the Importance of the Study of Physiology as a Branch of Education for all Classes," by James Paget, Esq., F.R.S.

the truth of the revelation which God has made, as to assume that truth and urge upon you the corresponding responsibility. Lent is scarcely a time for controversy; it is not a time to argue about Christ, and enquire whether He has spoken, so much as a time to be with Christ and to listen to His words; times for controversy there must be, and there must also be for us all, especially in the days of our youth, times of doubt, and of fear, and of anxious questioning concerning the revelation of God; how shall we wonder at this, when we remember that even Christ was tempted, and asked by Satan to renounce His allegiance? Still there are times when controversy may be hushed, and when quiet watching with Christ will commend itself to us as our best occupation, and when we may hope to lose sight of all anxious questionings in the sweet presence of Jesus Christ Himself. Hence, I say, that Lent is scarcely a time for controversy or argument, but rather for the earnest enforcement of those duties which arise from admitted principles and from recognised truths. Let us then take the Holy Scriptures in our hands, or press them to our hearts, and say, Here is the record of the way in which God has at sundry times and in divers manners spoken to our fathers by the prophets, and has in these latter days spoken to us by His Son; and having done this, then let us go on to ask ourselves what ought to be the practical consequences of having such a possession? It is a common saying in these days that property has its duties as well as its privileges, and so the possession of the Word of God, compared with which all other possessions must be poor and trifling, must bring with it very great duties: what are they? These, at least; to honour it, to love it, to strive if necessary, or even to die, for it;

but besides these, there is the more common and perhaps the more important duty, of exhibiting in our own
lives the ideal which Holy Scripture sets before us, the
duty of living like Christ, and becoming (as it were)
a living practical commentary upon the contents of
God's book. This is just the difference between this
book and others; other books you may read and forget,
this you must *not* forget; others you may have on your
shelves and not read unless you like, this you *must*
read if you can; upon others you may pronounce any
opinion you please, but this must govern your opinions,
and you must take it as the light of your feet and the
lamp to your paths.

Yes, this is the way in which you must treat the
Scriptures, not only for your own sakes, but for the sake
of others. I said just now that you must strive, if necessary, for the Holy Scriptures, but undoubtedly the
most effective way of defending them from assaults,
and making men honour them, is to act them out in
your conduct, and let Christ be revealed to men in your
lives. St. Paul speaks in the text of Christ being *revealed in him*. I have spoken of the force of that
phrase; and now, finally, I would ask you to compare
it with a similar phrase with which the Apostle closes
the chapter from which I have taken my text; he says,
"they glorified God *in* me [b];" they saw his life, they
saw the change made by God's revelation, and they
glorified God in him when they saw *Christ revealed in*
him; and so, Christian brethren, if we have received
a revelation from God, and if a deep responsibility is
laid upon us by the reception of that revelation, then
the best mode of discharging our responsibility is to
lead a holy and godly life. That will shew forth Christ;

[b] Gal. i. 24.

that will illustrate God's word. And depend upon it, that if the highest privilege that a man can attain is that God should be revealed *in* him, so the highest praise that he can attain is that men should be able to point to his holy, earnest, Christ-like life, and say one to another, There is a man in whom Christ is revealed, and in whom God is glorified!

SERMON III.

Personal Responsibility of Man, as individually dealt with by God.

—————◆◆—————

ST. MATTHEW xxii. 31, 32.

"But as touching the resurrection of the dead, have ye not read
that which was spoken unto you by God, saying, I am the God
of Abraham, and the God of Isaac, and the God of Jacob? God
is not the God of the dead, but of the living."

THIS is one of those wise and deep sayings of our
blessed Lord, which, while they testify to the truth
and inspiration of the Scriptures of the Old Testament,
tell us at the same time how much of profound, and
to some extent hidden meaning, lies buried beneath
the surface of the sacred text, unsuspected by the careless and superficial reader, yet not less surely written
for our learning, and forming a part of the lesson which
the Divine Author of the Scriptures intended that we
should draw from them. I say *intended*, though it is
probable that there may be some readers of this passage
of Holy Writ, who, while prepared to accept, as every
Christian is bound to do, reverently and submissively,
the interpretation thus put forth on the authority of
Him who spake as never man spake, may yet be disposed to doubt whether, but for that authority, the
inference drawn in it could be regarded as so certain
as it now claims to be regarded by us, or what there

is that makes it so natural and unquestionable as to call down upon the unbelieving Sadducees the accompanying rebuke, "Ye do err, not knowing the Scriptures." We may be sometimes tempted to ask, Might not the words of the Lord, spoken to Moses, be interpreted simply and naturally in a historical sense only, to recall to mind the favour shewn by God to Abraham, Isaac, and Jacob, while they were yet alive on the earth, to declare that the same God who had been their God during their earthly life would continue His divine protection to their posterity in the house of bondage ; without necessarily implying that the deceased patriarchs were still living to God, or containing a distinct declaration of the general resurrection of the dead ?

A doubt such as this, raised with regard to words which came from the lips of the Saviour Himself, would almost of itself suggest to the Christian student of Scripture a suspicion that the interpretation which gives rise to it, if not altogether erroneous, must be at least partial and incomplete ; that the true meaning of Scripture is not always that which lies on the surface of the text and suggests itself at first sight ; that the duty of searching the Scriptures necessarily implies the existence of truths within the sacred pages which only careful search can discover. The unbelieving Jew read the Law and the Prophets without perceiving that they testified of Jesus Christ : does it therefore follow that the testimony is not there, or cannot be seen there by those who read aright ? The unbelieving Sadducee read the passage of the bush without seeing in it any acknowledgment of an immortal life and a judgment to come. Yet a more earnest study might have shewn him that the testimony is there ; even as the Jew might have read in his own Scriptures that Jesus is the Christ. It is part of one and the same method in God's dealings with man, that neither His Works nor His Word will yield their proper fruit and do their full service to the creature on whom they are bestowed, without thought and labour on his part to avail himself of the hidden blessing. The bread that strengthens man's heart does not spring spontaneously in the field, to be gathered at once by every passer by; but needs to be cultivated with care, and wrought with labour and skill; and God has given to man the knowledge and the power by which this can be done. And if it is ordained that man shall not live by bread alone, but by every word that proceedeth out of the mouth of God, it is but according to the analogy of God's dealings with the body, if like labour be needed, and like means graciously provided, for preparing the food of the soul.

When we say, then, that a pious and thoughtful reader, though he were but a Jew, reading the Scriptures of his people by the light of the elder covenant, might naturally and rightly be expected to elicit from the language of my text the meaning which our Lord declares to be contained in it, we must presume that he would bring to the task of studying the Scriptures such aids as God had granted to him for the right interpretation thereof; such aids as are indeed, in a great degree, furnished to all men by the natural conscience and religious instincts of humanity, but which to the Jew in particular were enlarged and strengthened by the whole history of his forefathers and his race, and by the laws and institutions which guided his daily life and worship. Of these aids, the first and principal is that on which rests, as on its foundation, the possibility of any religious relation between God and man—the consciousness of the Personality of God, and of the Personality of Man. When God declares Himself, with express mention of individual names, to be the God of Abraham, and the God of Isaac, and the God of Jacob, He proclaims the existence of a relation altogether distinct from that in which He is revealed as having made heaven and earth, the sea and all that in them is, in which Abraham, and Isaac, and Jacob, and the whole race of mankind are included, with all the rest of the universe, with the mineral and vegetable creation, with the beasts of the field, the fowls of the air, and the fishes of the sea, among the wonderful works of God. The brute creation, indeed, are the objects of God's providence and sustaining care; but they are so as things, not as persons; they have no consciousness of any personal relation to God as *their* God; they have no feeling of dependence upon Him, prompting them to prayer; they have no sense of moral obligation towards Him, demanding obedience; they have no free-will to place that obedience in their own power; no choice to obey or disobey, making the one a duty and the other a sin; no conviction that there is a higher nature in what they ought to be than in what they are, and therefore a capacity, unrealized in this life, of a higher perfection and a nobler destiny. And therefore it is that the purposes of God's providence are fulfilled towards them when each successive generation completes its course, and accomplishes the period of its animal existence, and passes away from the earth, to be succeeded by another generation with a like purpose and a like end. Their permanence is of the species, not of the individual[a]: they glorify their Maker without choice

---

[a] Cf. Neander, "Life of Christ," p. 399, Eng. Trans.: "This argument, derived from the Theocratic basis of the Old Testament, is founded upon

and unconsciously; and therefore His glory is declared and His purpose is accomplished equally and without difference by this generation and by that; even as the grass of the field, which to-day is and to-morrow is cast into the oven, is clothed by God in each successive growth with each returning year. Man, too, as regards the mere animal conditions of his life, is subject to the same natural laws as the brute creation. Like them, he must pass through the stages of birth, and growth, and maturity, and decay, and death. Like them, he is subject to pleasure and, pain, and health and sickness; like theirs, his life is supported by the air which he breathes and the food which nourishes him. But the one prerogative which exalts him above the brutes; the one endowment whereby he is a person and not a thing, which places him in a personal and individual relation to a personal God is—strange paradox it may sound, but not more strange than true—that whereby alone he is capable of *sin.* It is, that God has given him a moral law and a free-will—a consciousness of duty with a power of obedience or disobedience, — in one word, a *responsibility.* By making man responsible for his actions, by giving him a power to do or not to do, and a sense of right or wrong as he chooses the one or the other, God has emphatically proclaimed to man, with a voice which all who choose to listen may hear, that the deeds which he does are not the consequences of the laws which surround him, not the results of the circumstances in which he is placed, not links in a pre-ordained series of causes and

a more general one, viz. the connexion between the consciousness of God and that of immortality. Man could not become conscious of God as his God, if he were not a personal spirit, divinely allied and destined for eternity, an eternal object (as an individual) of God; and thereby far above all natural and perishable beings, whose perpetuity is that of the species, not of the individual."

effects, of which every antecedent certainly and inevitably determines its consequent ; but acts which he performs as an author, not as an instrument, not as the machine, blindly doing the work which it is constructed to do, not as a portion of the universe, unconsciously fulfilling the grand law of the whole ; but with power to do or not to do, which makes the acts *his* acts,—the acts of an individual, not the consequences of a system. It is in no sense *my* act that the planets revolve in their courses, that the tides ebb and flow, that day succeeds to night, and summer to winter, and sunshine to shower. It is not even *my* act that the blood circulates in my veins, that the food nourishes my body, that my animal nature is subject to the periodical returns of hunger, and thirst, and weariness, and sleep. But when a temptation to sin comes before me, which I may yield to or may resist ; when an opportunity of doing good is offered to me, which I may grasp or let go as I choose ; these acts are mine and mine only : it is I alone who do them ; and in saying *I do them*, I pronounce myself a person and not a thing.

All this is implied, and its implication may be seen by every one who will look for it, when God selects, as He does everywhere and in every man select, some individual of the human race, Abraham or Isaac or Jacob, or you, or me, or our next neighbour,—we are all selected in our several ways and according to our several opportunities—and tells him, whether by external revelation or by the voice of conscience speaking within him, that He is *his* God and *his* Master; that He has a work for him, personally and individually, to do upon earth, which he may indeed do or neglect, but which is his business and no other man's to do, and for which he, and he alone, is accountable to God

as he does it or does it not. When God says, "I am
the God of Abraham," He virtually says this : "I gave
Abraham a command, and he, of his free-will, obeyed
it. I bade him leave his country and his kindred, and
he departed, not knowing whither he went; I bade him
offer his son upon the altar, and he stretched forth his
hand with the knife ready for the sacrifice." In doing
these things, and in the course of his life as God's servant, he shewed a consciousness of God's authority,
a will to obey God, a zeal to worship God, which, acting
imperfectly and partially in this life, among the lusts
of the flesh and the weakness of the spirit, and the
sins and backslidings from which no man in this life
is free, yet gives sure and certain promise, in its yearn-
ing after better things—in its consciousness of a more
perfect obedience than it renders now—in the struggle
between the flesh and the spirit which marks a higher
nature, hampered and hindered as yet from fulfilling
its calling, and giving complete exercise to its powers—
of a future and more perfect obedience, of a closer union
between God and man, when the corruptible shall have
put on incorruption, and the mortal shall have put on
immortality.

It is true that this grand prerogative of man has its
terrible as well as its glorious aspect ; and its terrors
are emphatically expressed in that one word, *Responsibility*. If it is glorious to know that we are not mere
passing phenomena, coming and going in the course of
the world's development, mere links in a chain, impulses
in a movement, bubbles rising and bursting in the great
ocean of time, but that we have a personal, individual
relation to God, not in time only, but in eternity ; it is
no less terrible, for a being deeply conscious of sin, conscious, in the very consciousness which convinces him

of his immortal destiny as an individual, and in proportion to the very intensity of that conviction, how immeasurably that which he is falls short of that which
he ought to be—it is terrible, I say, for such a being
to know that all this sin, all this shortcoming, is his
own personal act; that the power from which it springs
is the very self and essence of his own personality; and
that for all that proceeds from that source, he himself
—the very personal self—is accountable in the sight
of God, and will be called to judgment hereafter. So
terrible is this thought, that it is one of the commonest
and most successful resources of the Tempter, to avail
himself of this terror to steal men's consciences from
them by the most effective, the most fatal device by
which moral sense can be lulled to sleep, and man's
whole being entranced in a fool's paradise of delusion;
a device which does not merely betray men to sin in
single acts, but moulds their whole life upon the dream
that there is no sin and no judgment. Philosophy
(such is the imposing name which it usurps) is called
in to persuade men that this sense of personal responsibility is itself a delusion; that man, like the
things which he sees around him, is not an individual,
but part of a system, moving in the course of that
system, governed by the laws of that system; a patient,
and not an agent in the world; an instrument, and not
a workman; a thing, and not a person. It is a delusion,
not like the coarser seductions of vice, addressing itself
to one passion or one appetite alone; it has its various
forms, adapted to men's various temperaments; it has
its snare for the noblest as well as for the meanest
elements in our nature : it aspires to special sway in an
age when those nobler elements are most active, and
among souls the most conscious of their presence. Not

merely our animal cravings and lusts, not merely the
frivolous desires of vanity and the light allurements of
pleasure, lend themselves to this deception; but our
intellectual and spiritual endowments, the very principles which, in their due place and within their due
bounds, are most beneficial and most ennobling; the
far-reaching inquiries of science—aye, and even the
heaven-aspiring emotions of religion, may be made fuel
to feed the flame which consumes godliness and manli-
ness alike out of the heart and life of man. In some
natures it takes the form of a mere idle pursuit of the
pleasures of the moment, a careless, aimless existence,
in which the strong determination of will, the steady
consciousness of purpose, are surrendered for the roving
vanity of a butterfly enjoyment of the passing hour;
and the person becomes a thing in obedience to his
impulses. In others it appears as a so-called rational
conclusion, erecting itself on the pride of intellect,. and
feeding itself by misuse of the discoveries of science.
Man sees the material world around him governed by
fixed laws, and exhibiting an unbroken connection of
antecedent and consequent: he penetrates the secrets
of nature, and subdues her forces to his service by dis-
covering everywhere, as his researches penetrate further
and further, one and the same type of immutable law
and order: and his pride whispers to him, "May not
this my discovery, which explains so much, explain all
things? Have I not unveiled the secret of the universe,
my own nature included? Are not human actions the
fixed consequence of motives and circumstances, even
as wax is melted by the fire, and water congealed by
the frost? Is not man's law as theirs, man's responsibility as theirs." Thus, like vanquished Greece of old,
the captive makes a captive of its conqueror. The pene-

trating intellect, the resolute will, which have made brute nature their vassal, are content to bow themselves down to the level of that which they have subdued ; and the person becomes a thing in obedience to the prejudices of a theory. But again, the same self-deception, the same morbid longing to escape from personal responsibility, may take a higher ground still, and delude to its own purposes a yet nobler element of human nature. Even the religious feelings may be made to co-operate in the destruction of their own vital principle and source ; and the personality of man may complete the sacrifice of itself upon the shrine of an external authority, acting in the name of God, but not after God's manner,—not as the loving Father, but as the despotic Master. There are some minds which seem to find a soothing charm in the thought of entire self-surrender to some infallible authority relieving them from the solemn responsibility of working out their own salvation with fear and trembling ;—an authority which claims to speak clearly, distinctly, unerringly, where apostles and evangelists have spoken with stammering lips and uncertain sound ; which whispers soothingly in the ear its tale of a servitude which is better than freedom, of a blind obedience which is better than moral action. " Pause not," it says, " deliberate not, question not ; only submit. Be an instrument in my hands, a servant to execute my commands, without doubt and without hesitation ; and lay upon me the whole burden of responsibility for thy right action here, for thy eternal salvation hereafter." The scientific delusion addressed itself to the logical side of man's nature, to lead astray the active, penetrating intellect : this, the religious delusion, addresses itself to the emotional side of man's nature, to the amiable, sensitive, delicate feelings, to

the taste and the imagination which feel without
reasoning ; to the sense of dependence upon a higher
power, which within its proper bounds is religion, and
beyond those bounds is superstition.   It is not now
the hard, pretentious, arrogant demand of so-called
science ; it is the gentle, delusive persuasion of a siren
singing a dreamy soothing strain, till the will and the
conscience are lulled to sleep under the charm, to awake
no more, or to awake when too feeble to resist.   It
is a dream not the less dangerous for being pleasant ; not the less deadly for the charms of fancy that
gild it :—

> " For like the bat of Indian brakes,
>   Her pinions fan the wound she makes,
>   And soothing thus the dreamer's pain,
>   She drinks his life-blood from the vein."

The life-blood is indeed drained when the sense of individual responsibility is destroyed.   No man can be
a moral agent by deputy : no man can be saved by
deputy.

It is, no doubt, a source of false comfort, very pleasing to the indolence, or cheering to the timidity, of
those who are unwilling or afraid to take upon them the
burden of responsibility which God has been pleased to
lay upon them, to think that the necessity, or even the
possibility, of free volition and self-determined action is
taken from them by the intervention of some necessary
law or some infallible guide, which will relieve them
from the duty of thinking and acting for themselves, or
even will merge their apparent self-action in a necessity
by which all accountability is abolished.   Yet the whole
analogy of nature, as has been conclusively shewn by
the great master of this method of reasoning,—the whole
course of God's treatment of man, as manifested by the

conditions which He has made essential to the very existence of human society, shews beyond all reasonable
doubt, that man's position in the sight of God, as regards natural religion also, is that of a free agent, accountable for his personal actions, not that of a portion
of the physical universe, governed by physical laws [b].
And the same argument from analogy, if applied also
to revealed religion and the institutions based upon it,
shews with equal clearness that it is a contravention of
God's purpose towards man, an anomaly opposed to the
whole method and scheme of the Divine Government,
to suppose that He should, in this instance alone, have
designed to set aside the free-will and personal responsibility of the individual, by the interposition between man and God of an infallible guide, armed with
authority to become accountable in each man's stead.
It is not thus that God deals with us in the general
course of His Providence, whether manifested in nature
or in revelation. The laws of nature, like the truths
of revelation, are in themselves sure and stedfast and
unchangeable and free from all error; but man, in his
interpretation of those laws, in his attempts to apply
them to his own individual case, is ultimately dependent
on his own judgment, fallible though it be; and is made
to act on his own responsibility, however momentous may
be the consequences [c]. God has permitted laws of science
to be established by human research,—laws which are
of undoubted truth and authority when rightly applied;
but in the actual application of them, they are guides
and aids only, not masters; assistants to, not substitutes
for, the personal judgment; acting with, not super-

[b] See Butler, Analogy, part i. ch. vi.
[c] Cf. Whately, " Essays on some of the Dangers to Christian Faith," &c.
Essay IV. sect. 5. Sermons (1854), p. 318.

seding, the responsibility of the individual. The laws of chemistry and of mechanics are fixed and unchangeable; yet a slight mistake in the mixture of ingredients for a chemical experiment may cost the life of the operator; a slight miscalculation of the power of his forces, or the strength of his materials, may lay the mechanist, mutilated or dead, beneath the ruins of his own engine. How much better, men are tempted to say, would it have been, had God given to man an infallible guide to prevent his very pursuit of knowledge from being turned to his own destruction. Better indeed, as erring man would dictate to the omniscient God; but God has not given us such a guide; and therefore we judge more wisely and reverently if we conclude that it has been withheld because it was better for man that he should not have it; because the evil of such a gift would have overbalanced the good.

If we turn from nature to revelation, we see the same method of God's dealing with man. Why, asked the heretic of old, did not the Creator contrive some certain means to save man from falling? Could a Being of perfect goodness and wisdom and power have been unable or unwilling to prevent sin from entering into the world? Because, was the reply, man's likeness to God consisted in his free-will and power over his own acts; and God's goodness is more shewn in bestowing on man this excellent gift of freedom, than it would have been had he been made obedient by subjection to a servile necessity[d]. Does not this shew how precious a thing in the sight of God is human freedom, that even sin and death were suffered to enter into the world, rather than that the majesty of that freedom should be violated? Nay more: when God Himself, in the form and nature of

---

[d] Cf. Tertullian, *Adv. Marc.*, ii. 5, 6.

man, came into the world which He had made, to save His people from their sins, did He accomplish His warfare against evil by cramping the will of man and enforcing obedience to rigid rules and minute observances? Far from it. He censured those who sat in Moses' seat, for laying on men's shoulders heavy burdens and grievous to be borne[e]: He abolished in His flesh the law of commandments contained in ordinances[f]: He lovingly invited men of their own free-will to take upon them His light yoke and easy burden[g]: He taught by figures and parables, by general precepts and principles, whose particular application to his own case each man must make for himself:—above all, He conveyed the best and highest teaching for meditation and practice, not in the rules of a code, but in the example of a life.

And does not each one of us, if he will but consult honestly and faithfully the witness in his own heart, feel that God is dealing with him, too, as an individual, called upon to work out his own salvation, to resolve as an individual, to act as an individual, to be saved as an individual? Does he not feel that, whatever aids and supports in the path of duty God may have been graciously pleased to grant to him— the precepts and examples of parents and friends, the free use of the Bible, the services and ordinances of the Church—all these aids in religion, like the analogous aids in nature, must co-operate with, and be appropriated by, his own free-will and personal responsibility, working with them throughout his life, even to the end? Does he not feel that there are daily placed before him opportunities of action, occasions of choice to do or not to do, the decision of which rests with him-

---

[e] Matt. xxiii. 1—4.   [f] Ephes. ii. 15.   [g] Matt. xi. 29, 30.

self and himself alone, in which no example of others, no associations or habits, no laws or customs,—no, nor even the Church of Christ herself, can relieve him from his immediate, personal, individual responsibility? Have there not been occasions in his life when passion, or prejudice, or predilection, or persuasion, or terror, have tempted him for the moment to strive to get rid of this burden of responsibility, to cast himself into the stream of some reckless course, to be carried onward unresistingly by the current; and when some seeming accident, some real interposition of God's Providence, has compelled him for the time to pause and act for himself, has placed God before him as *his* God, guiding *him*, reasoning with *him*, expostulating with *him*, speaking to *him*, as it were, face to face, as a man speaketh unto his friend? God's government of man in this world is made up of general laws and special providences mingled together; and neither is complete without the other. If law, and system, and rule be manifested, not merely in the labours of his temporal life, when he sows his seed in the ground, that the crop may ripen by the ordained influences of soil and season, but in his spiritual life also, when he acts upon or is acted upon by others, in accordance with the general principles by which motives, persuasions, exhortations, examples, are recognised as forces influencing human conduct; there are no less moments, and those too lying at the very core and centre of his religious life, when he is withdrawn from all these influences, and enters into his closet, and shuts his door, to pray to his Father which is in secret, with the prayer which none but himself can offer; when the *I* and the *Thou* which mould each petition and each thanksgiving, each utterance of an individual need, each acknowledgment of an individual favour, shew that the freedom and personality of finite and fallible man never so truly assert themselves, as when, instead of being overwhelmed and crushed down, they are quickened into fresh life and vigour by direct communion with the Almighty and Allseeing Personality of God.

SERMON IV.

Personal Responsibility of Man, as to his Use of Intellect.

ST. MATTHEW xxi. 28.

"Son, go work to-day in my vineyard."

NOT only the higher graces of the Gospel are gifts, not only does it require a special revelation to man's spirit, to open the eye of the soul, to impart faith, to restore the knowledge of God, and to bring out all the higher parts of our nature; but Holy Scripture shews us that what belongs to an inferior part of us, viz. the intellect, is likewise a direct gift from God. This you may call natural, the others supernatural. Thus we read of the artists of the tabernacle being specially endowed, though their work was chiefly in cutting of stones and carving of wood.

Solomon obtains, as a special gift from God, the ability to be a good ruler. The seventy elders, who are called to help Moses administer justice, are qualified by a gift of the Spirit. Some of the gifts, mentioned in 1 Cor. xii., are partly intellectual—the word of wisdom, the word of knowledge, teachers, helps, governments.

Now we know that it is a great temptation to human nature to forget that our personal endowments are gifts. Few strong muscular men consider that their physical prowess is a gift, for the use of which they must give account; that they are not at liberty to let themselves out as prize-fighters, or to seek only admiration, or to overtax their strength ; but that their bodily powers are given them to earn a living, or fight for their country, or protect the weak, or to fit them for work as missionaries, or, in some other way, should be turned to account, and used to the glory of God.

So is it with mental gifts, not only with that specifically called intellect, but with imagination, memory, sympathy, discernment of character, tact, eloquence, and the like. God gave them, God may withdraw them; they may be used rightly, they may be used wrongly ; like others of His gifts they may be developed and improved by exercise, or they may wither from disuse ; they do not stand alone, but are related to God's other gifts. Intellectual gifts are used amiss when the possessor, forgetting God, employs them merely selfishly, to fight, for instance, his way to renown, or when his only object is to excel this one and surpass that other, and to be the topmost man in his year, his set, or his profession.

It is not well when men argue, not for truth but for victory ; when, whatever opinion is advanced, they are always clever enough to start objections, to pick holes, to bring forward what can be said on the other side, often making the maintainers of truth look foolish, by overbearing their well-meaning dulness with the bright sallies of glittering sophistry.

It is not well when the gifted man is always engaging in a series of gladiatorial feats, determining that he will be the oracle of his circle, putting down all who contest his supremacy, and measuring swords with every new comer, in order to be esteemed the best master of his weapons.

It is not well when the powers of the intellect are concentrated on money-making, or the acquisition of professional skill, irrespective of duty, as if man had only to please himself, do what he liked, was his own master, might do what he would with his own.

It is not well when men indulge in intellectual freaks, take up some hobby, spend the labour of a life on some pursuit which gratifies only a whim of their own, and does not advance human happiness, or do good to their fellow-creatures. How many a record of misapplied intellect do the libraries of this University contain! Parish priests, who should have been instructing their simple flock, shutting themselves up in their studies to write books that nobody reads, acquiring perhaps a little fame in their own families or small circles, but neglecting the humbler, but more useful work they were set to do. How many a fanciful problem, many a useless investigation, has been pursued, with no small amount of intellectual ability, because self-conceit prevented a man from listening to advice, or self-will diverted him from his own proper business.

Nor less is it an evil when a man overtaxes his intellect, sets it to do more work than it was meant to do, forgets its relation to the other parts of his nature, prides himself in it, as if it were the only valuable power he possesses, and ends perhaps by exhausting himself, so that, in after life, he is able to do less good work than others.

Alas! when we think how intellectual gifts may be abused, we are reminded that many of those who are most mischievous in their generation are the most gifted, intellectually. There are strong minds which can solve hard questions, capacious brains which can hold multitudinous details, clear heads which can illumine difficulties, acute intellects which can detect fallacies : and these are great powers for good or evil. They are sometimes used to propagate mischievous theories, to sap Christian evidences, and exaggerate Scripture difficulties.

Before now, these have been the men who have tried to banish theology, to secularise education, to vulgarise mental philosophy, to introduce materialism and utilitarianism, to make so-called useful knowledge every thing, to appreciate nothing but intellect, to deify man, to despiritualise nature. These cold, hard, powerful, unloving intellects are very dangerous. Unhappy the times in which they are the ruling spirits ; unhappy the nations on which they impress their characters, and whose institutions they are allowed to shape or remodel.

But let us look on the brighter side, the good that may be done with intellectual gifts.

In every age intellect has much influence; perhaps, in ruder ages, bodily prowess may somewhat eclipse it, but, in a state of society like ours, its weight is especially great. It is not indeed the only thing that gives a man influence : personal appearance, goodness, cheerfulness, moral qualities, are greatly influential, but intellect is necessary in many situations, and useful in all. It is a beautiful thing to see it applied to advance human happiness, discover remedies, explore the works of God, justify His ways, explain His dealings, vindicate His truth, interpret His Scriptures, extend His kingdom, and apply His Word to the heart. It is delightful to see a man use his intellect to refute error, maintain truth, right the oppressed, and to solve the difficult questions which a complicated state of society produces. It is pleasing to see versatile abilities, like the elephant's trunk, available to take up a small matter,

nimble enough to do a poor man a service in a petty
difficulty, and robust enough to remove a great obstacle
from a nation's progress. Power of intellect is not virtue, it is only strength, which may be applied to a good
purpose or a bad. Thank God we have seen it combined with piety in humble philosophers, in great theo-
logians, pure poets, holy painters, reverent enquirers,
philanthropic physicians, and by them applied to do
God's own work on earth.

Now let no one think that, in treating of the use of
intellect, we are addressing only a select few, and that
no one can profit by the subject but those who are,
obviously and pre-eminently, intellectual.

On the contrary, it is a duty incumbent on the servant and the peasant, as well as the accomplished
student, to improve themselves, to cultivate the gift
given them, be it little or be it much. If a person
cannot read and write, they should try to learn to read
and write ; if a person, a little better off, does not know
English grammar and history, they should improve
themselves in those subjects. Each should have an
ideal before them, and should not sit down contented
without striving, with God's help, to reach that ideal.
He who is going to be a lawyer, should think what an
accomplished lawyer ought to know. He who seeks
holy orders, what a clergyman ought to understand.
Each should set himself, while he has the opportunity,
to cultivate himself to the required degree. Now it is
very common for persons to improve themselves from
worldly motives, in order to get on in the world, in
order to qualify themselves for a better place, in order
to avoid being laughed at for errors ; but what one
desires to see is, persons improving themselves that
they may be more useful to their fellow-creatures, may

E.

fulfil the duties to which they are called, and may re-
commend religion. Oh that we could see the children
of light as diligent as the children of this world; that
we could see as much done for the glory of *God* as
for *self*-glorification.

Alas, well-meaning people are often very indolent,
and so become incompetent, mismanage matters, and
are superseded by those who have less principle but
more ability.

Let us remember that intellectual gifts are commonly
given small at first, so as to be capable of enlargement
and growth, they are improved by diligence and application, they are increased to the industrious and pains-
taking: on the contrary, they are withdrawn from the
indolent. And for our encouragement let us remember
that in the nature of things the good Christian has many
advantages, even intellectually; he is saved from that
arrogance and self-conceit which hinders a man's learning; he is strengthened against those sensual temptations which enfeeble the intellect. He is more able to
work with others, than those are who are selfishly thinking only of what they can carve out for themselves.
Besides this, God has so constituted human nature that
all good things are connected together, help each other
forward, and play into each other's hands. The truths
of religion, besides their adaptation to the highest part
of man, his spirit, furnish food also to his intellect, and
the best food too. The contemplation of God is the
key to unlock the secrets of the world in which we live;
all things fall into their place, for the man who knows
the centre round which to arrange them. The Christian has many of the first principles of philosophy involved and implied in his creed; he has, therefore,
some real intellectual advantages over others.

But he has to use his opportunity *betimes*. There are periods of life after which it is difficult to acquire new ideas. Perhaps each period has its special aptitudes, and if these are wasted, they cannot easily be recovered. Thus the memory is strong in children, it is easy for them to learn by heart, difficult for most of their elders. So the faculty of learning to speak a foreign language is impaired after a time. The young man, again, is poetical; the faculty deserts most men in after life. The young man, again, takes an interest in everything: as we grow older, we grow narrower, are disposed to mind only our own business, shrink into our shell, leave new fields to be explored by others, become less adventurous and less vigorous.

What follows from this? why that the young should understand that the present is the time, in which they are making or marring themselves. We are all little aware of the consequences of our actions; a *child*, we will say, is idle and does not know that unawares he is deciding his profession; he is unable to pass a particular examination, and his parents must alter his destination. A little later, when grown to be a young man, he is idle, or he misapplies his talents, uses them injudiciously, with self-will, in self-chosen paths; and the consequence is, that though he knows it not, he is deciding his place in his profession, his influence on society. From not having brought out the muscles of his mind, he will become unequal to difficult questions, he will be gradually left behind, the age will move on, and he will be voted antiquated. He will be eclipsed by persons who have not had his advantages, but had native mother wit, sharpened by practice, and, while they are energetic and successful in propagating error, he, who ought to have been the advocate of truth, is unable to do justice to the side he maintains, and is overborne by those who would have been his inferiors, had he been decently industrious, and availed himself of his opportunities. How often is the orthodox, but feeble, indolent Churchman thus discomforted by a pushing opponent, who has had little education, but has made the most of what he had.

I have said something to remind you of responsibilities with regard to intellect. You are not to let the powers of your mind lie dormant, while you are absorbed in bodily exercises, as if you, by preference, were giving yourselves to toils which gamekeepers and fishermen get their living by. There is but a short time in which you can learn, there is much to be learnt. Much harm will be done, if you prove incompetent to the duties which will devolve on you; you are on trial when you little think it; men are often deciding about us when we think there is nothing of importance going on. They see we shall not suit them, they judge us below the mark; and the secret of our shortcoming is, that we pleased ourselves, when we ought to have been labouring for God. " Son, go work to-day in My vineyard," is the call He addresses to many. Like a kind earthly parent, He is really seeking our good, when He sets us to do work for Him. The son will have the benefit of the ground he is cultivating for the Father.

"Son, go work to-day in my vineyard ;" every word is important. Go in a filial spirit, as a son, who will be tenderly regarded by an indulgent Parent; work "to-day," put not off till to-morrow; "work," not play over it ; work with brains, if that be thy calling, " in my vineyard," in improving thyself, that thou mayest improve others. In My vineyard work for Me, not for thine own credit. " Go," do something at once, begin, take a step.

He knows your powers, ask what He sends you to. He has given you gifts, provoke Him not to withdraw them. Let every sad case of aberration of mind, softening of brain, temporary eclipse of intellect, read you a lesson, lest from you, too, the talent be withdrawn. Hide it not in a napkin, but put it out to the best account: "Occupy till He come," He who will surely reward: who will say, "Well done, good and faithful servant, thou hast been faithful in a few things, be thou ruler over many things;" few things now, many things then. Yes, they are "few;" the brightest achievements of genius, wonderful calculations, astounding discoveries, feats of skill, triumphs of art, imagination that electrifies, wit that enchants,—what are they to the gifts which shall adorn the elect, when they shall have outgrown the infancy of this state of existence, and no longer speak as children, understand as children, think as children, but shall have become truly men and have put away the childish things of this state of existence?

Meanwhile, the brilliant achievements of intellect here should be looked upon as of value, even to the rudest peasant, the least developed savage, because proofs of what belongs to the race, promises of what their nature shall be capable of in other worlds, where man shall be restored to the image in which he was first formed, and the divine intention in creating him shall at last be satisfied.

Brethren, this is a Lenten subject, for two reasons; first, it suggests penitence for the misuse of powers, neglect of opportunities in times past—for the idleness of boyhood, the self-will of youth, the failures of manhood, for not having made as much of ourselves as we might, for labouring, when we did labour, rather for our own credit than for God's glory; and, secondly, it suggests exertion ere the night comes when no man can work.

O that some might be moved from this day to adopt as their motto what the Saviour revealed as His own principle, " I must work the works of Him that sent Me." Realise that you have a mission, that it is a mission to *work*. If a man will not work, neither let him eat ; he will not eat, in the sense of enjoying healthy life, deriving nutriment and exhibiting growth ; he will be less able to do work, he will dwarf himself, he will dwindle ; he will be rejected as a wicked and slothful servant in the great day of account, when the Lord, having returned, having received the kingdom, shall command His servants to be called unto Him and shall reckon with them.

SERMON V.

Personal Responsibility of Man, as the Possessor of Speech.

ISAIAH vi. 5.

"Then said I, Woe is me! for I am undone: because I am a man
of unclean lips, and I dwell in the midst of a people of unclean
lips: for mine eyes have seen the King, the Lord of hosts."

TO-NIGHT I am to ask you to consider the great
gift of speech, and the responsibility it brings with
it. Like the coins which we daily pass through our
hands without reading the superscription or testing the
metal, we use language for our momentary needs without thinking whence it came to us, nor what is its worth.
Words! What are they after all? We use them without thought, we twist them into jests, we combine them
into the speech or the poem. They are the handy
interpreters of every day's wants; when we have no
wants, they are the convenient toys that amuse us with
our friends. Who can find any solemn side to such
a subject? Who, that does not exaggerate for an effect,
can attach much importance to the use of speech? But
words are a great gift of God to man. Preserved in the
strata of the language we speak are all the monuments
of our history, and you could tell whence our people
came and what they believed, what virtues they ranked
high, what vices they glossed over. The names we use
are often the sole monuments left to us of some forgotten theory of morals, or physics, or medicine. And

this reminds us that our language is our inheritance
from the ages that are gone; it grows richer as generations pass from the accumulations of their thought.
Descending to us, it educates us; for the ideas which
animated our fathers in their struggles, in their aspirations, pass into watchwords which recall and excite
the same ideas in them that use them. And the sound
of such words, before they are quite understood, stimu-
lates us to apprehend the fulness of their meaning.
Such words as faith, and truth, and freedom, contain
almost a moral system. To know them fully, we must
ourselves have learnt to trust in God, and to yearn for
truth, and to value the protection of equal laws; to
know them fully, we must know something at least of
the history of those whose blood, poured out for the
sake of the faith that they professed, became the seed
of the Church that bore a hundred fold, of those who
step by step wrested from various forms of tyranny the
rights which have made our persons safe, our property
secure, and our nation the envy of those who have not
advanced so far in the same conflict.

But if language does so much to fashion us, it is an
instrument for us of wonderful power in moulding other
minds. I do not mean now that the great masters
of speech can sway the passions of mankind, or soften
their affections, or convince them by force of reason.
This is obvious, but it concerns us less. I mean that
all speech, the common currency of a place like this, is
an instrument of power, whether we have measured its
power or not. Most of us have not thought of estimating
the power of a thing so common and so familiar. But
the mightiest forces that actuate the world are those
which are unobserved, because they are so constant.
The thunder makes us tremble with awe, though the

storm after all only smites a chimney or a tree. The earthquake is a whole world's wonder, though perhaps it only swept away a few cottages. But the gentle breath of the air, which no one notes, is the life of man and beast; taint it, and the whole earth will reek with pestilence; withdraw it, and every living thing will die and vanish into dust. And the sun, which rises daily to run its endless course, gives life and growth to plant and animal; and the slow current which sweeps over the Atlantic unnoticed, bearing with it the genial warmth of another climate, tempers the air for us, and disperses the chilling fog, and makes our isle endurable. It is so with the power of speech. It is common as the air we breathe, as the sunshine which we welcome, as the water that washes our shores; but it is mighty in operation, it is universal. It never sleeps. The hum of many voices rises from the earth continually, and rises not in vain. God's work, or else Satan's work, it is for ever doing. There is no hyperbole in those words of St. James which perhaps we have been accustomed to construe as if there were: "The tongue is a fire, a world of iniquity: so is the tongue among our members, that it defileth the whole body, and setteth on fire the course of nature." Let us for a few minutes consider the great power and responsibility of the gift of speech. Amongst our companions words are cheap enough, and we think only of saying what may please their taste; before our God, who means us to be, in our way, prophets and preachers of His truth by all we say and do, our speech is an awful gift. We need God's presence to shew us *how* awful: "Woe is me, for I am undone; because I am a man of unclean lips, and I dwell in the midst of a people of unclean lips: for mine eyes have seen the King, the Lord of hosts." Oh Lord of Hosts, be with us to-night, that these words of the prophet may sink deep into our hearts for Jesus Christ's sake.   Amen.

Let us then consider this matter not as an abstract question, but in the way that becomes us, in connection with our own shortcomings.   We speak that which we ought not ; we fail to speak when we ought to speak.

If we were to decide what was the commonest fault of the tongue amongst ourselves, we should almost all answer that it was the making light of sin.   We can allude to any sinful act in three ways : we can speak of it as the Bible speaks, as a sin against the pure and holy God ; or as prudent men of the world speak, as a mistake, and a blunder, and a want of self-command and dignity ; or as the thoughtless speak, as something to be laughed at and forgotten, a natural and admissible thing.   Our language is copious enough for any of these.   Let me take one set of cases in which it makes the greatest difference which of the three tones we adopt.

In such a society as this place contains, one of the greatest dangers to souls is impurity.   The temptation is strong at a time of life when the passions are turbulent and feverish, and the ruin, when it does come, is complete.   For so it is, that that sin which is palliated sometimes as being manly, does involve in a great ruin all the noblest parts of manhood in us.   Those that worship this idol are fit for nothing else.   The delusion is so engrossing that it leaves room for no other feeling. It makes the heart hard beyond all other sins.   The steady light of family affection which burns in the breast of many a. young man, cannot subsist amid the fierce glare and stifling fumes of passion let loose ; it flickers and disappears.   Serious studies become impossible ; pure wholesome nourishment is savourless to

a palate accustomed to stronger stimulants. It draws
in one by one all other sins to become its ministers.
Intemperance in meat and drink have some secret re-
lationship to lust. Deceit is often wanted to compass
its ends ; it is more ready than any other sin to smite
with cruel treachery the face turned up towards it in
trust. When lust came in, even a David's noble spirit
fell into utter disorder ; even a Solomon's wisdom
could not save him from idolatry and shameful indulgence. Laziness, and fear, and a dislike of physical and mental effort are invariable consequences ;
the blood-guiltiness into which David fell is far from
impossible. And then follows that pitiable state in
which, athwart all serious labours, all innocent recreations, all prayers and solemn assemblies, flit the unclean phantoms of a heart still going after its covet-
ousness. The passions were indulged, that after
a season they might be restrained, and the serious
pursuits of life might replace them. But they will
not be dismissed ; their breath is poison, but they
were sweet to us. They were the soul's first choice,
and to the last they will stick to it. We try to build
up a new life, the most respectable, according to the
strictest laws of prudence ; but prudence is not strong
enough for the demon that has possessed us. The
temptation comes back at some unforeseen moment,
and the artificial structure of our life topples down
into the old folly, and delusion, and uncleanness. Or
say that true repentance comes, and our eyes are
opened, and, according to the northern fable, the faces
of our sins that seemed so fair, are seen, as they de-
part, to be mere hollow shells or masks. We pray
that God will give us a clean heart, and renew a right
spirit within us. But our hatred of the sin is not com-

plete. Then, when we confess and bewail it, we tremble lest it should come back again, and we should view
it complacently, with something of its old charm. Into
the very presence of the King, the Lord of Hosts, our
sin may pursue us, and we, poor weak broken creatures, may be obliged to yield to it for a moment even
there, in that presence. Oh, state of sin and punishment in one! to stand there where we know so well
that sin is death, and yet to be a prey to fits of lingering love for sin.

From this powerful temptation men are protected
by a triple defence; by natural shame; by a feeling of
conscience, that as all sin is enmity against God, this
is in an especial manner an offence against His holiness;
and in the third place by fear of the punishment hereafter which is so plainly affixed to this class of sins.
"If any man defile the temple of God, him shall God
destroy; for the temple of God is holy, which temple
ye are[a]." The poor tempted soul, about to leap into
this abyss of sin, sees the depth of the ruin into which
he is going; and shame, and fear, and the love of God,
hold him with strong bands, and will not let the strong
temptation pluck him down.

What shall we think, dear friends, what shall we say
of one who in that moment of trial when a soul is sus-
pended between life and ruin, steps in, with no interest
in the case except the love of evil, to unloose the
bands that hold him to life, and so to help his down-
fall? If there is any retribution for sin, is not this the
sin to call it down? Ah, it is so common! Only a few
words from a skilful tongue, dropped once and again,
and the ruin shall be. Well may the Apostle say,
"Let no man deceive you with vain words: for be-

[a] 1 Cor. iii. 17.

cause of these things, [the sins of the flesh,] cometh the wrath of God upon the children of disobedience [b]." The words are vain words, but they deceive. Tell him that modesty is weak and boyish, and that a certain measure of dissipation befits the finished character of a man. Disconnect this sin, in all that you say about it, from every thought of God; speak never of fornication and adultery; language is rich in words that soften and disguise the guilt of this sin. Shew how common the sin is. Throw on nature and on youth the blame, if there is blame, of passions too strong for restraint. You will extinguish, by such means, the last spark of that shame, which, fostered in a home where all was pure and chaste, has been sustained till now from extinction by a mother's pure prayers, by her solicitous efforts to keep enfolded even when far off, her darling in the invisible arms of her chaste affection. You will succeed. It were better that a millstone were hanged about your neck, and you drowned in the depth of the sea, than to reap such an accursed success against one of those for whom our beloved Lord died. You will have broken the natural armour against the sin, natural modesty; and nothing that you could do could ever make it good again. You will have helped to make a breach between him and God; for He knows well, even if you have forgotten, that "this is the will of God, even your sanctification, that ye should abstain from fornication [c]." In the silent night, and at moments when the passions are cool, conscience, prescient of the judgment, says within him, "If any man defile the temple of God, him shall God destroy."

Could these results come from a few thoughtless

[b] Eph. v. 6   [c] 1 Thess. iv. 3.

words ? Yes. " Behold, how great a matter a little fire kindleth [d] !" Like those murderers lately, who, to release a prisoner, blew into ruins a whole street, you knew not the power of the fire you kindled. But you knew there *was* fire ; it is your sin. Had you spoken a word for God instead of pleading against Him ; had you uttered your abhorrent protest against fleshly lust ; had you done less even than that, and when the talk turned towards things forbidden, had you turned it towards something pure and lovely, towards the studies that ennoble the mind, or towards those domestic ties and affections which clear away as by magic, from any soul not yet corrupt, the grosser thoughts of sin, you might have done just this, you might have saved a soul alive for God.

2. And this brings us to another peril of the tongue. Two of the safeguards against sin are the love of God and the fear of judgment. But they suppose a faith that God indeed is, and that He verily is a rewarder of them that diligently seek Him. A theology of suppositions has no force as a safeguard. You cannot say to the heart, " On the hypothesis that there is a future life, you would do well, as a matter of calculation, to live for it, because it may be true, and then you are safe ; and if it should not be true, then you have done no harm." Faith may be strong or weak, but it cannot be faith and not faith at the same time. Through this state of division and doubt men have sometimes had to pass, but to linger in it is death. It is not a phase of religion, but a suspension of it. There is much doubt amongst us, but some of it is the troubled doubt of those that strive and seek the truth, and pray

[d] James iii. 5.

for light, and some of it is an acquiescent doubt, content to part with its convictions, and to put a vague sentiment of religion in the place of the truths that have been assailed. And all truths are assailed: whether God is a hearer of prayer and a defender of them that trust in Him; whether Christ is God indeed, and His Cross is powerful to save a lost world; whether we shall live after we cease to breathe; whether the idea of duty is anything more than an enlightened calculation; whether sin is guilt or only mistake: criticism does not shrink from opening all these questions. If there be any one so unhappy, that his mind is in doubt about them all, there can be no faith of any kind possible for him till some of the doubts are cleared away. He for whom nor God, nor Christ, nor conscience, nor the life to come are realities, has nothing, without him, on which he may support himself. St. Paul says, "I know whom I have believed,"— that is the avowal of faith: this man says, "I know nothing in which a man may believe." I do not bid such an one to despair; but there is one duty for him, paramount to every other,—to look for light, to pray for light. Like the traveller lost upon a winter's night, he must know that to wander is not death, but to lie down in his wanderings is to be frozen and to die. But how are these questions, this state of doubt, treated in common talk? People mean no harm when they jest about the last new theory in science, or shew a little learning by quoting the last new book that argues that matter is eternal, and claims for man an enormous antiquity, with the drawback that myriads of years were spent in passing out of apehood into manhood. They mean no harm, yet when they come to consider what is the tendency of the conversation

in the circle in which they live, they may have to
confess that its tone tends to encourage doubt, and to
make them content with the darkness.   There is this
special mischief in all idle talking, that the general
thoughtlessness that pervades it, or the general vice,
is greater than the vice or thoughtlessness of each
particular speaker.   "The tongue is a fire."   The jest
about Holy Scripture, the argument against this truth
or that, the ridicule of one religious practice or another,
kindle other like remarks; and so all religion is ban-
ished from the conversation, albeit each speaker had
left in his own heart some point of belief, some ray of
hope, or at least some traces of fear and shame.   There
never was a time, there never perhaps was a place,
where it was more needful to be wary and circumspect
in what we say about religion.   Inquiring minds, vexed
and anxious themselves, go about to gather what comfort they can from others : they count the votes, as it
were, that are given around them, for Christ and against
Him.   Mocking words fall from you about sin, about
the Bible, about the Lord; and you are silently recorded thereupon as of those who have thought it good
to part with your belief.   Yet speak, if it be only for
pity, the better thing that is in you.   You pray sometimes, or you abhor the thought that man's existence is
rounded off complete when he dies, with no eternity to
follow; or you have looked on the face of Jesus in the
Scriptures and cannot call that Man, that life, other
than divine; at least you do not think religion should
be dealt with by jibe and sneer.   Season, if but with
a grain of salt, the vapid worthlessness of the irreligious
talk, and your vote will then be recorded the other way.
You have something left still.   When all seemed going,
you have found something to hold fast by.   He, too,

that listens, will tighten his grasp on the something that he still possesses, and will hold it fast.

Might not even our religious conversation be more fruitful than it is? St. James, from whose Epistle we might derive a complete code of rules for the government of the tongue, says, "Let every man be swift to hear, slow to speak, slow to wrath: for the wrath of man worketh not the righteousness of God." He is speaking of religious things, of hearing and speaking "the word of truth," mentioned in the former verse. Does not religion suffer often from our hot and impetuous advocacy? We are zealous for God, and that, we think, excuses everything; and we are ready with the nickname or the good story against those whose views differ from our own, and we separate readily from those that will not go so far as we; and the lines that separate Church parties are daily more deeply marked. We meant to do what was righteous before God; our fault is only zeal. But "the wrath of man worketh not the righteousness of God." God's great purposes, in the growth of His kingdom, will gain nothing from our noisy warmth. Our righteousness before God would be to speak the truth, but to speak it in love; and to be slow to speak, lest perhaps we should utter the word of poison instead of that of truth. All have suffered something in this heart-searching time. It is a great misfortune if those that are firmest in the faith should disfigure the beauty of it by a want of love. You despise the gainsayer of your truth; you denounce him; you see in him nothing but stupidity and perverseness, and you tell the world so. Yet he is your brother after all. Your Lord could pity that perverseness and stupidity which kindles in you so much irritation. Is there, after all, anything more moving to a good man's heart

F

than the fact that many are losing sight, from one cause or another, of Christ their only guide? The world was redeemed not by fiery indignation, but by a manifestation of unspeakable love. And what was true of our redemption is still true. No man is ever reclaimed from an error by mere rebuke and anger. Go to your Lord in prayer at this holy time, and say to Him, "Lord, we have kept Thy faith :" "Well done, good and faithful servant !" "Lord, we have been indignant against those who kept it not ; we have smitten them, and degraded them, and brought them into disrepute :" "Put up thy sword within thy sheath. The wrath of man worketh not the righteousness of God. Judge not, that ye be not judged."

Great is the power entrusted to us in speech ; and all too careless are we in the use of it. In this place, some fifteen hundred souls, created by God for immortality, are educating each other constantly by speech and by example. You are careless about this familiar gift ; you think that your share of it matters but little for good or ill. Think not so. All the hours of social intercourse from end to end of the year are passed in conversation. You claim no peculiar right to advise your friends. But whether you are always blotting out the lines that mark off right from wrong, whether your heart is stirred and your tongue kindled by frivolous and worldly subjects only, whether the sneerer at religion or the filthy talker can count on your smile in answer to his jest, whether you are ready at all times to turn others away from things useful and lovely and of good report, towards frivolity ; or you seek the contrary of all these, makes a greater difference than you can compute. Of the difference to you we need not speak ; it is a difference as between death and life.

But your power upon your hearers has been great. Oh, that our dear Lord, who was willing to be called " The Word," because He was the revealer of the Father to us, would teach us how to follow Him, as in all things, so in this! We, too, may reveal whatever of the power of God has been manifested in our souls to those among whom we live. Woe to us if we do not reveal it! " By thy words thou shalt be justified, and by thy words thou shalt be condemned." Awake, thou that from idleness or false shame hast thought it useless to govern thy tongue. Be a messenger for Christ. Banish bitterness, and wrath, and anger, and clamour; put away filthiness and foolish talking. Refrain thy tongue from all evil. Assured at last that the gift entrusted to thee is great and excellent, be more watchful in its care. Above all things, pray that Christ Himself will be wisdom to thy mind and lips, that the tone of all thy words may be such as He would have thee utter, that thou mayest catch something of the boldness of His zeal, tempered always with the tenderness of His compassion.

SERMON VI.

Personal Responsibility of Man, as to his Use of Time.

ST. JOHN ix. 4.

"I must work the works of Him Who sent Me, while it is day.
The night cometh, when no man can work."

WHOSE world are we living in, our own or God's?
Who is master of our being, ourselves or God?
To whom are we to give account of our being, to ourselves or to God? Questions, all very simple to the
understanding, but which we answer practically, in exactly the opposite way to that which we in theory and
in words acknowledge. We confess, daily, most of us,
to Jesus, "We believe that Thou shalt come to be
our Judge." We follow that confession by the implor-
ing cry, "We therefore pray Thee, help Thy servants,
whom Thou hast redeemed with Thy Precious Blood?"
We sum up our prayers for pardon for sins, for mercy,
by all He has done, merited, suffered for us, with "In
the Day of Judgment, Good Lord, deliver us." We cannot say a Creed without confessing our belief, that He,
now our Redeemer, shall hereafter be our Judge. The
belief remains on our lips; we hold it in our understanding; does it enter into the texture of our every-
day life? Supposing that, by God's grace, we have been
kept to-day from anything, very notably wrong, does
it occur to us that "to-day" will have anything to do

with our eternity? Well, it may be startling, that this one day (if there have been nothing in it markedly against the will and grace of God) should have to do with our eternal doom. Look back, then, to yesterday, or to many yesterdays, or to weeks past, always supposing that there have been no marked deadly sin in any of them, nothing which should, unrepented of, separate you from God, and destroy your spiritual life; nothing, in which you shall have taken a marked part against God's law, and have chosen the wages of the Evil one, present pleasure and eternal death. Granted your time of life, the buoyancy natural to it, the recreations, amusements, merriments, lightheartedness, which, in measure, no one would, at your age, wish to interfere with, so they be innocent, is there still nothing, which should, you think, influence your eternal being? But does it then come to this, that, but for those marked sins, of which God says that "they who do those things shall not inherit the kingdom of God," we need have no care, no anxiety, no thought about eternity?

To take the seeming ways of the mass of mankind, one could have no doubt that they think so. Here and there, *one* seems to be aware that lesser acts lead to greater of the same kind; that repeated acts form habits; that custom gains an iron power over the will, until a man, by misuse of his free-will, almost destroys the freedom of his will, to be recovered only by some strong effort or some mightier accepted grace of God. But, for the most part, if one were to ask any one, why he did any given thing, except just the actual necessary duties of his state of life, without which a person could not live or attain the temporal end which he wished for, the honest answer would, I fear, be, "because I like it." In other words, a man's own will is, with certain great exceptions, the rule and measure of his acts; and, to judge from men's ways of speaking, Almighty God and he have each very good reason to be satisfied with the distribution. Almighty God gets His fair share; perhaps, more than He used to do, or more, may be he thinks, than others give Him. Almighty God has his prayers, morning and evening; some prayers (I fear for the most part not very many) in the Chapel-service; then on the Sunday, God has anyhow twice in the day his bodily presence (wherever or however occupied his mind may be, for, I fear, a notable part of the time), a poor man has a shilling every now and then; and then, in the day, he gives a certain number of hours (very few, I fear, unless ambition has its share in the arrangement) to the cultivation of his mind. For the rest, who disputes his right to it? It seems as if the impious flattery of the Roman poet, when the weather cleared in the morning for the Imperial spectacle,—

"With Jove divided empire Cæsar sways,"

were the religion of Christians, and that over ourselves at least we hold a partnership of jurisdiction with Almighty God. Of course, to make this not Atheistic, it must be put in the form, that Almighty God has waived His absolute right over us, that He has substituted for this His unlimited dominion over us, a sort of feudal sovereignty, in which, we holding this His earth, or our portion of it, and our time in it, as a sort of feof from Him, are bound to render Him certain limited services, to withhold ourselves from doing Him certain very limited despites, and that, these being either discharged or deferred (well is it, if the payment of God's dues is not deferred to some unknown period beyond our power, at the supposed end of life), then over all the rest we are to be seized as lords, and it is resented as a very unreasonable and unjustified, and almost monstrous, demand, if any one put in any claim, on the part of God, as to any portion of this wide heritage which we hold of Him.

Of course, we have no intention to be Atheists. We speak respectfully of God, as far as we know of Him. He is the Great First Cause of all things, Who made our first father, Adam, some 6,000 years ago. He made this earth which we inhabit, whether with any distinct thought of us, geologists leave as a question in abeyance. He upholds us all somehow in being; whether by unvarying laws which He made at some time heretofore, people do not define to themselves. He is very great, and when people are in trouble, they betake themselves to Him. People can with difficulty, or cannot altogether, escape the idea of judgment. But then by whose rule? Tacitly or avowedly, men mean their own. From the "I am no worse than my neighbours," by which the poor man satisfies his conscience amid the thought of death and judgment, to the "God cannot punish what belongs to the nature which He made" of the self-justifying dissoluteness of the rich; they mean, in fact, "we will not," (or to speak respectfully,) "we shall not, we will not have it, that we shall be judged, otherwise than we will."

"Responsibility!" the word is almost clean gone out of our common language, except that we speak of the "responsible minister of the Crown," in the sense that the Sovereign has to give no account of her acts to man; and a "responsible" person or firm, is one which can discharge his or its monied obligations; and we can understand that *that* responsibility must be complete to the very last farthing. How is it, that we can

so discern our relations to this world, and, in the midst
of the light of the Gospel, not discern our relations to
Almighty God?

And yet this would-be quasi-independence of God,
if it were true, what a miserable lowering of our whole
being it would be! For what would it amount to?
Simply to this, That as to a large range of our being,
we were beneath the notice or care or thought of
Almighty God; that what we did or did not do was
too insignificant for Him to heed; that He left us to
battle (for battle we must, if not with sin, with misery
in this stormy world), and set no more store by us,
than we do on the uptorn weed, cast on our shores by
an angry sea, unless indeed men make use of its decay
and corruption to manure their fields. Wonderful dignity of man's would-be independence, to attain, in his
own idea, to this, that he is held of too little account
by God's infinite Wisdom to be regarded by Him; too
mean, for Infinite Love to love him; too puny, for God's
Infinite Majesty to stoop to elevate him; too limited,
for Divine Intellect to communicate Itself to him, to
enlarge him; too worthless, for Divine Greatness to heed
whether It have or have not his service or his love.
Miserable as it is false, and proving itself false by the
misery to which it would abandon us!

The true dignity of our nature lies in that relation
to Almighty God, which involves the minutest responsibility. We, all of us, think or have thought something
more highly of ourselves,—it has added (whatever our
standard was) dignity to our estimate of ourselves, to
find ourselves an object of interest to one who was our su-
perior in whatever our standard of eminence was,—pure
intellect, or maturer knowledge, or ripened thought, or
even this world's rank; and, if they bestowed individual

unpaid-for pains in developing our powers, we not only felt grateful to them, but a certain responsibility in corresponding to their pains.

Faint shadow all, all human love, care, thoughtfulness, of the ever-present all-comprehending love of God, of which it too is (though one of the least) a fruit !

This is the true greatness of man—to belong to God, enfreed by God to become freely the slaves of the love of God. For the inconceivable greatness of man is, to have been made by God for Himself; to have been made by Him, Who Alone is Greatness ; Alone, Goodness ; Alone, Wisdom ; Alone, Majesty ; Alone, Infinite Love ; nay, Who Alone Is ; and Who, being Alone the Source of being, Alone can bestow true glory and greatness ; and the glory and greatness which He bestows, must be in some created likeness of Himself, since there is no ideal greatness and goodness and glory out of Himself, for which He could form us.

The only adequate object of existence is to exist for God. The only adequate pattern of perfection which to copy, is Almighty God, or God made Man ; Man, Who was therefore perfect, because He was also Almighty God. The one unvarying interest *in* this life, or *of* this life, is that God cares for us, God loves us, God, Whose Being is ever to communicate Himself, Whose mode of existence within Himself is in a continual communication of Himself,—the Father to the Son, and the Father and the Son, as One, to the Holy Spirit, Who is the Bond of Both,—has created us, to whom· to communicate Himself ; that He wills that we should be little likenesses of Himself; and, lest we should lose any or all of the perfection which He designed for us, watches as well as guards us so minutely, is so jealous that nothing out of Him should divide our

hearts with Him, supplies us with such graces, visits us
with inspirations, appeals to us by calls and re-calls
and re-recalls, immerses us in Sacraments, provides a
fresh Sacrament anew for us for every fresh fall, will
not let us go, lest we should miss the end for which
He created us,—Himself.   The measure of our greatness is God's care for us, His protection of us against
ourselves, His anxiety to preserve us for Himself.

   This is the great end of our being, to be won by correspondence to Divine grace,—the possession of Almighty
God.   God has willed to make us, not like the Angels
to whom He unveiled His glory at once, and left it
to them to choose or to refuse Him, to exist, each in
that separate order in which He had created them.
To us, whom (it is the common Theological opinion)
He created to fill up their ranks, broken by the fall
of those who fell, He has given an almost immeasurable
power of progress.   Progress, the love of which, well or
ill-aimed, is the ruling principle of all but stagnant
minds, is our perfectibility.   We have no choice but
progression or regression.   And this progression is by
us here unimaginable.   For we see something of some
of the qualities which gleam through men's looks or
words ; we see a supernatural light illumining what is
of earth.   But what the sum of all shall be, what relation all shall bear to the sitting on the right hand or
the left of Jesus in His kingdom, it is reserved for the
Day of Judgment to declare.   We know of an especial
nearness of those who shall sit on the twelve thrones,
judging the twelve tribes of Israel.   We know of that
Virgin-band who follow the Lamb whithersoever He
goeth.   It has been said of more, I think, than one,
that God had revealed that he was for his burning love
received among the Seraphim.   But, even as it is One

in our nature, Who is for ever personally united with the Godhead, so—above all the highest creatures, whom God either has or ever will create, in a special dignity and nearness, one and alone, (even as the Incarnation, God made Man, is one and alone,) must *she* exist, with whose flesh God the Son willed that His Flesh should be consubstantial, whose flesh He in His own deified, whom on earth He willed to obey as His own Mother. This dignity of unspeakable nearness to Himself, He, plainly, ever predestined for her, and in one instant He bestowed it on her : but by what giant progress in graces, by what undeviating correspondence to Divine vouchsafements in time, must that soul have been formed, to whom, in her fourteenth year (it is thought) was vouchsafed the choice which, by Divine grace, she accepted at the risk of shame and reproach, that of her, ever-Viigin, should be born the Saviour of the world, her God. Yet her Son pronounced her more blessed for her obedience than for her Mother's care of Himself. This progress, from the lowest scarce-saved soul to that Throne which is most encompassed by the effulgence of the Divine, has but one limit—time. No bound is there to the rich accumulated succession of Divine graces ; no limit to the intensity of the Divine power of grace, except our grace-acquired, grace-gifted, capacity to receive it; no term to the development of our capaciousness to contain God, except this, that growth must be in this life, in time. After this life, if by God's mercy we attain, is the everlasting fruition of God, in that degree, to which by Divine grace we have been enlarged in this life. But growth is no more. Ever-enlarging knowledge of the Infinite Wisdom of God there will doubtless be ; ever-unfolding will be the treasures of Divine love. But as, here, we are men, not Angels ; and as Angels are not

Archangels, nor Archangels Cherubim or Seraphim, or
Thrones, or Dominions, or Powers, and as each Angel is
thought to have his own special perfection and beauty,
so we shall each, in all eternity, remain that special
soul, which here we, by our use of the grace of God in
time, became.   At the great account, we are to receive
according to the deeds done in the body, whether good
or bad ; then are the five or two talents to be bestowed
on each, according to our faithfulness in cultivating
whatever God has entrusted to us.   Paul, glorious as
he will be, he to whom to live was Christ, he, by whose
mouth Christ spake, he, in whom Christ inworked, whom
He empowered mightily, will be evermore that glorious
spirit which, by God's ever-inworking Spirit, he became,
(whom may we, though afar, behold, and joy in his joy
in Christ !) ; but he will be evermore that, which through
his zeal and sufferings and love of Christ he in time
became, and no other.   John, too, will be there, with
all that love which he drank in when he lay on Jesus'
bosom, which he drew, hour by hour, from the love of
Jesus Who loved him, and still more perhaps from that
martyrdom of threescore years and ten, during which
his soul was parched with thirst to behold again his
Lord and his God, Whom he loved.   Yet is he the same
John, who, through that long privation of the sight of
Him Whom his soul loved, was formed for the eternal
love of God and Jesus.   There is Peter, with his soul
of fire, through whom Jesus first admitted both Jews
and Gentiles into His blessed fold ; his soul on fire with
all that love, which the look of Jesus kindled in him
when fallen ; love, augmented all his life long by his
penitent remembrance of the occasion of that love, by
his loving joy in partaking of the sufferings of Christ
and his loving faithfulness in feeding His Master's sheep,

anew committed to his care. Yet is he the same, which by all that fiery zeal and love, penetrated through and through by the Spirit of God, he became.

This, then, is the measure of the value of time, the possession of God, the greater or lesser possession of Him, Who is all Goodness, all Wisdom, all Beauty, all Sweetness, "the Fountain of all knowledge, the Fountain of eternal light, the Torrent of pleasure," the all-sufficing Beatitude of all creation, yea, of all possible creations. For He may be possessed in an all-but-infinite variety of degrees, infinite to us, who have no measure by which to measure them ; degrees, as far removed from us as the furthest star, whose light has visited this earth, is in space ; yet all infinitely below the infinity of our God. But in this all-but-infinite range of beatitudes, there is a growth almost unbounded, so that even if we have chosen God Alone for our Portion, we might still, by His grace, rise as much above what we are, as Heaven is above earth. For there are no limits to the might of the grace of God, except those which we ourselves put to it ; no limit to the height, Alps over Alps arising, to which each formerly-attained height seemed like a dead plain, except our lingering in the plain of the devoted cities, when Angels' hands are leading us on, yea, when the Lord of the Angels bears us up by His pierced Hands, bids us tread safely on the lion who would devour us, and beats down Satan under our feet.

Did you ever see any one perfect ? The blessed Saints of God knew that they were not. The graces, which God most worked in them, seemed to them the most imperfect, because in them the film was most cleared from their eyes, and, though through a glass darkly, they saw something of the perfection of God. Everything which is in earnest, is striving toward perfection ; everyone who is in earnest, finds that it is not here, that here are but the germs ; the flower and fruit will, we trust, through the Blood of Jesus, unfold in eternity. Yet such as is the germ here, (well, if there be no canker !), such will the flower be in eternity.

We all seem to ourselves to have energies, which are never completed here. We all seem to have a work to do, of which, at best, some fragments only are wrought out here. Year by year, all life long, we have to lay aside aspirations which we once had ; works, for the glory of God, we have to leave undone for ever ; the pyramid, which we would build for God, narrows as life goes on ; well is it for him whose building has least of wood, hay, stubble in it, or is broken off the least unsatisfactorily !

But these things, though evidences of the value of time, do, except as far as they are ensouled by the love of God, and the pure purpose of serving God in them, belong to time only. The eternal loss or gain of that power of loving God, which God, in His eternal love, desired that we should attain, is for eternity.

Sloth, then, as a deadly sin, is a far more comprehensive, terrible, almost irreparable evil, than most of us have been apt to think of. Sloth, as mere idleness or want of exertion, is, in your seed-time of life, a greater disqualification to serve God hereafter, than you can now be aware of. No one is aware of the value of anything which he is wasting, while he is wasting it. The almost irreparable loss opens our eyes. Powers of mind, which are not developed in the due period of their development, are probably stunted for life. Habits of accurate thought, which are not formed then, are probably lost for life. Each period of life has its own appointed work; and it is rarely allowed to any one, to make present time do the work of the present and the past at once.

Idleness is also, as you know, proverbially called "the mother of all the vices." It is Satan's own enclosure, his own special country, where he hunts and ensnares souls. Not relaxation, but relaxedness is a peril of souls. Relaxation, which is to fit for dutiful exertion afterwards, may be used to the glory of God, in thankfulness for the exuberant buoyant strength, which it vents, as much as the repairs of the daily decays of nature, which the Apostle instanced as a thing to be done to His glory, or as we may lay us down to rest in Jesus. It is well known how a Saint, when asked what he should do, if he knew that our Lord would come that night to judge, said that he should finish what he had then begun; for he had begun it for the glory of God, and for Him he should finish it. Yet what he so meant to finish was an ordinary game, certainly more used in his country than in ours by such as would lead lives devoted to God. It is not, then, what seems to some of us, even an undue measure of relaxation, which we should dread for you. We may dread that the habits of boyhood may be prolonged unduly into manhood. But this is scarce an evil. Be what you will, so that you retain the innocence and purity which belong to boyhood. Genuine gladness of heart is well pleasing to our Good Father, Who giveth us all things richly to enjoy, Who has decked His creation with gladness, the ray of Whose light transmutes the dullest things of earth into a radiance of almost heaven-born joy.

Think not, it is joyousness of soul which loyal duty to your God could interfere with. How should it, since "love, joy, peace," are first-fruits of His out-poured, in-dwelling Spirit? It would transmute, engolden joy, not damp or quench it. How should rebellion against God spice joy? What joy is there in unseemly jest, or coarse ribaldry, or half-uttered, half-hinted filthiness, or in-solence to the Name of God or to His Word?

But the deepest fear for you, the deepest fear for us all, the all-comprehensive fear, is, not as to the waste of portions of time, but one universal waste of all. Much of life must pass in nothings. Waste seems to be a great law of this our world below. God scatters a profusion of His choicest gifts, and nothing seems to come of it. Sleep and its attendant offices mostly take one-third of our lives. Then there is in other ways the daily recruiting of nature's daily decays. Then the intercourse with others, what fruit brings it? employ-ments, which we cannot call directly wrong; but what comes of them? The strongest brain cannot be ever at work (the worse for us, if it could), and we must per-force relax. What good is there in it all, even if we escape sin? If we are intellectual, our brains become little encyclopædias of a variegated knowledge. We forget far more than we remember; and what we do remember, what use can we make of the greatest por-tion of it? Solomon, whose wisdom the Queen of Sheba came from the ends of the earth to hear, sums up his own experience: "Of making many books there is no end, and greedy study is weariness of the flesh." What a life of fiery zeal it was, which Elijah summed up: "It is enough; now, O Lord, take away my life; for I am not better than my fathers!" Truly, if no more came of it all than we see, life were one waste. To see evils, and to be powerless to remedy them; to see men steering a goodly vessel, with precious merchandise,

G

straight upon the rocks, and counting it good service ; to call, and there is none to answer; to labour, and the winds are contrary; what would this life be, if one counted the body of this life only, but labouring for the wind ?

But where, then, is the soul of this life? This it is which made me speak of the risk of one universal waste of time. For since, to us individually, time is that portion of days (few or more) which we live here on earth ; and since the only adequate end of this life is to gain Him Who made us for His boundless bliss and love ; and since He wills to communicate Himself to us in eternity in an almost infinite variety of degrees, according to our capacity to receive Him ; and since our capacity to receive Him will vary endlessly, according to our use of His grace here, the power of love which we have acquired, the conformity to His blessed Image, the God-inworked likeness to God ; then all of time, all of life is lost, in which a man does not lead the supernatural life of grace, does not grow in the capacity of loving God.

This is the soul of every outward act, of every word, of every thought. It matters little what the body may be. It matters nothing whether it be the most menial act performed on this earth, or the highest intellectual achievement, whereby a God-gifted intellect unlocked some secret of God's creation. This is the body still, to be transfigured by the grace of God. The sun which illumines and gladdens this our orb has no more, if so much, relation to God, as the poor worm, which is trampled upon and dies. Even the meanest thing done to God, is of countless price ; any, the most magnificent work done for any end out of God, is absolutely worthless.

This, then, is the one secret of life, this its one un-
dying interest; this alone gives unity to life, this alone
makes life not objectless; this is abiding reality amid
a world of shadows; this endures, while all around
perishes,—to live to God. It may be, so thou art not
living in sin, thou wouldest not have to change one
outward act, certainly not one outward employment.
The body would remain the same, at least in its great
outlines. The studies, if they are right now, would be
right still; the recreations, if they be innocent now'
would continue still. Not the outward things would
be changed, but thou. For such as a man's love is,
such is he. And him thou lovest, for whom thou doest
whatsoever thou doest. If thou doest them for ambition, for pride, for vainglory, for vanity, for human
opinion or praise, these are thy gods; they are thy
reward. "Verily, I say unto you, they have their reward;" have it, our Lord says, wholly to themselves [a];
have it, not again to have it; have it to themselves in
time, not again to have it in eternity.

Dost thou them for God? God, ere thou hast done
them, has laid up thy purpose among His treasures.
When by His grace, thou hast done them to Him,
thy act is stored up for thee, to be rewarded in the
Great Day.

Is God too little for thee? is He too low an object
for thy ambition? is His Wisdom too narrow for thee
to covet? is His love not fiery enough to kindle thy
soul? God has made thee individually to be the
object of His love. He created thee, when He might
have created millions of beings less unworthy of His
love. He created thee, with the whole good-will of His
Infinite love resting on thee alone. He redeemed thee,

[a] ἀπέχουσι.

G 2

as if there were no other to die for.   He imparts Himself to thee as individually as if He were not the sustenance of Angels, the Life of all which lives.   What craves that Almighty Heart of love but that thou shouldest return Him love for love, that thou shouldest, in all eternity, have larger outpourings of His love?   This, then, is the measure of the value of time, eternity of infinite love, proportioned to the love thou bestowest here upon thy God.   Empassioned love here does everything as would please the object of its love.   Thou wakest, morning by morning, with the love of God overstreaming thee.   Give thyself for the day, thy thoughts, thy words, thy acts to His love ; to speak words or to leave them unspoken, to do acts or to leave them undone, as thou thinkest in thy truest heart, that thy God, Who loves Thee, in His love for thee, wills for thee.   Thou lovest thyself only with a finite love ; God loves thee with infinite love.   We love ourselves with a blind love; God loves thee with an infallible love.   Oh ! it will give such a deep interest to life's dullest monotony to do those monotonous things to thy best, according to the mind of God ; no time will be heavy to thee which shall upbear thy soul to God ; no employment will be dull to thee, in which thou mayest approve thyself to God (nay, the duller, the more interesting, because in it there is less of self, and so, more safety that it is done to God).   It will be a joy to thee to repress the half-spoken unseemly word ; for thou wilt have gained the larger capacity of love of God.   The men of this world would think it a token of madness if anyone had strewed along his path the glorious lustre of precious stones such as are pictured in the heavenly Jerusalem,—diamonds, pearls, carbuncles, rubies, amethysts,—and he, neglecting these, were

to treasure up shreds of hay and straw ?   But now they
are not precious stones of any passing lustre, to which,
if so thou dost, thou preferrest the dry hay and stubble
of this parched, perishing life.   They are priceless pearls
of purest beauty which thou mayest gather, not to form
any crested coronet, but whereby thou shalt thyself
shine with the Divine Glory, the beatific Presence of
the love of thy God.   Remember Him now ; remember Him in these His redeemed, now restored to His
love [b], and He Who will not remember thy sins will remember thy love, and will repay thee with Himself,
thine own beatitude for ever, thine own God, to be
thine own for ever.

[b] For a penitentiary.

SERMON VII.

Personal Responsibility of Man, as to his Use of Money.

ST. LUKE xix. 15.

"He commanded these servants to be called unto him, that He might know how much every man had gained by trading."

FOR the subject of this evening's thought and this evening's warning, my brethren, I have taken these words from our Lord's parable of the Pounds, not as though the gift entrusted to the servants in the parable in any way necessarily implies the gift of money, any more than it does so in the cognate parable of the Talents. In both parables, as we all know well, the talent or the pound stands for any of the unnumbered trusts which the bounty of an all-wise Father has committed to our hand. For all alike are we responsible, in that all alike are His. But, although the pound or the talent represents not *exclusively* the gift of wealth, it certainly does include it; and there is that in the use and abuse of money amongst ourselves which makes the words specially fitting to-night. For there are two leading thoughts running through this parable,—the thought of our stewardship in time for that which will bear fruit in eternity; and the thought of the account which the return of the great King will bring with it.

"Occupy till I come," is the condition attached to every external gift of God: "That He might know what

" every man had gained by trading," sets forth the responsibility under which we are taught to carry on that occupation, and to discharge that trust.

Of course it would be easy to carry out this principle into every department of the various callings in life; but to-day's subject limits us to one of the entrusted gifts. I suppose that there never was a time when men needed more the cautions and warnings which tell of the snares of riches, or the promises attached to their lawful ministration; never a time when the burning words of Isaiah, or St. James, or our blessed Lord Himself, needed more to be spoken in ears dull to listen, and to hearts already callous through the hardening power of money misapplied.

I. For if there be one characteristic of our own day, which distinguishes it from any which have gone before, it is the rapid increase of material wealth. For the first time in the history of the world the laws which govern the accumulation of wealth have been in our day a recognised science. To speak of such an increase as though it were a great evil, would be as weak and foolish as to complain of the advance of scientific discovery and the unfolding of nature's secrets. For in the first place, nothing is more unwise, or less likely to lead to good results, than to be ever complaining of the days in which we live; and next, the gifts of the natural world, including that of wealth, come of the same hand as the gifts of the kingdom of grace. Still, the fact itself is noteworthy, and we have not surely been left without warning as to the dangers and temptations incident to such an age, or as to the responsibilities which follow upon such gifts. Many of these a thinking man may gather for himself; upon some of them the Word of God itself has spoken.

II. And in the second place, as there never was a period of greater wealth, so never was there an age of greater poverty. Never before were Dives and Lazarus brought into closer contact. The reasons for such a condition of things we may leave to the economist; the political remedies to the statesman. But here again the fact is noteworthy. Misery and squalid poverty abound and overflow hard by the highway of palaces; starving thousands teem in all the great centres of human industry. These are the *contrasts* which meet us daily, and never more prominently than at the present moment. However the statesman may look at these things, for the Christian heart such a phenomenon must have its lesson.

III. And once again, a worse result yet remains behind: I mean the portentous increase of luxurious living among those to whom money has been committed—an evil which has spread far below those whom we commonly term the wealthy classes. Self-indulgence in its more refined and therefore in its more seductive forms, personal sloth and indolence, a shrinking from the hardness which goes to make up the manly Christian character, sometimes even a theoretic speculative defence of such luxury, as though it really were the end of human life—this is a phase of society which in this place, at least, no one will deny to be on the increase; which no thinking Christian man can fail to deplore. Account for it how you will, the fact remains. The great gift of God (for it is His gift still), the great gift of God, His blessing on the material wealth of England, has resulted through the unfaithfulness of its recipients in two most deplorable issues—the greatly increased luxury of those to whom the wealth has been committed; the greatly increased misery of those from whom in His providence it has been withheld.

I trust that, speaking at such a season as this, when self-knowledge ought to be bearing fruit in self-denial, such thoughts as these will not be met and stifled by any one with the impotent commonplace defence which we mostly encounter in the world. I trust, further, that speaking to Christian hearers, I may assume two certain unquestionable positions on these matters: first, that the gift of money is a gift of God; and secondly, that as such a gift, it is to be occupied for the Master's use. There are higher truths than those of the economist, and deeper principles involved in the constitution of society, than the accumulation and distribution of wealth.

This evening's subject has to do more with the use than the acquisition of money. I am speaking most likely to some at least who have had little to do with its acquisition, but have something to do with its distribution; to some, probably, who are learning their experience as to money's value and money's use. It is a lesson, like most other lessons of life, to be gathered by experience; and, like most experimental lessons, it involves some loss and some suffering in the process. Still, Christian principle may rule in the expenditure of small incomes in young hands. We may not expect one on the very threshold of life to be an accomplished economist, but we may reasonably look for care and for self-denial as from those who count themselves the stewards of the Lord Jesus Christ.

For we may be met, and continually are met, with this answer, "We have but little to spend, and little "opportunity for waste; warnings about the danger of "riches belong to others, we are not exposed to their "fascinations." If some such thought comes across your mind, put it away as a mere blind and deceit. So do we find in a country village; every member of the congregation will refuse to apply the parable of Dives, and all count themselves to be in the blessed condition of Lazarus, because they are mostly poor men, and one or two only of the whole number fare sumptuously. And so one class after another shifts upwards the burden, and no one fits it to his own shoulders, no one being in his own estimation a rich man; each one, according to the old definition, counting "enough" to mean something more than you have got.

My brethren, this is one of the devices of the tempter, by which he seeks to blunt the sharp cutting edge of the Word of God. Experience in ministerial life will tell you, as it has told some of us already, how easy the plainest and most direct teaching of Holy Scripture may be thus rubbed off. We should tell our flock that Dives was not condemned by reason of his riches, nor Lazarus saved by reason of his sores; but that faithfulness or unfaithfulness to the gifts committed to us, be those gifts great or small, is the only test of our stewardship. So specially of the gift of money. We may run off upon the excuse that we are none of us rich men, that we have just enough for our needs, and not always that; and so we may lose altogether the sense of our responsibility, forgetting that the owner of the one talent was arraigned before his lord's tribunal; and the one talent, hidden and profitless, was the cause of his condemnation, when they that had five and two entered into the joy of their Lord.

As practical teaching upon the uses and abuses of money, let us take two passages of God's Word, one from our Lord's own mouth, one from that of His Apostle's. St. James in very solemn words, which our age of all ages has need to take to heart, condemns the heartless unproductive expenditure of his own day: " Your silver and your gold is cankered, and the rust

"of them shall be a witness against you : and shall eat
"your flesh as it were fire. Ye have heaped treasure
"together for the last days[a]." On the other hand, our
blessed Lord's encouragement comes to aid us in the
use : "I say unto you, Make to yourselves friends of
"the mammon of unrighteousness; that, when ye fail,
"they may receive you into everlasting habitations[b]."
Both verses are full of help, the warning and the consolation. For it is a consolation to know and to believe
that as money is the gift of God, so the possessors of
money may, if they try, find a way of making the miserable dross, which turns to the condemnation of so
many, abound to the increased happiness of the possessor through eternity.

I. And first, of St. James's condemnation. How may
we be heaping up treasure, evil treasure, utter condemnation, for the last day? In two ways surely : in
reckless expenditure on ourselves, in ignoring and putting aside the wants of our fellow-men. Both are the
crying sins of our generation ; both may be the sins of
those who, it may be, have not overmuch to spend ; both
are habits fostered in early days. "To live in pleasure
"on the earth and be wanton," "to nourish the heart as
"in a day of slaughter," is of course the special temptation of those who have just begun to learn what the
satisfaction of spending is, and have not yet learned its
responsibilities. The day comes in after life most surely,
if we be thinking men at all, when the remembrance
of old spendthrift habits and reckless self-indulgences
does "eat the flesh as it were fire." As of other sins, so
also of this, which at the time you little count for a sin,
the bitter ashes remain in the mouth when all the sweetness of the apple of Sodom is departed. The days of
hardness, it may be penury, family cares, and the sweat

[a] St. James v. 1.   [b] St. Luke xvi. 9.

of the brow bring home vividly enough the truth, that, even in this life, we inherit the sins of our youth, God in His mercy giving us the grace of penitence, even though it came too late to undo the wrong.

And side by side with personal self-indulgence ever goes the heartless neglect of other men's needs. An age of excessive wealth is, I said, an age also of exceeding poverty. Here again however the economist may reason and explain, to the Christian heart it is a terrible and ghastly contrast. It is a contrast, too, all the more telling to those before whose eyes it is presented, just because they, who ought to be most keenly alive to it, are for the most part wholly unconscious of its existence. Multitudes walk the streets of our crowded cities all their life, in the pursuit of business or pleasure, with all the appliances and enjoyments of wealth, all unconscious of the seething mass of ignorance, vice, and misery only a few yards from their own homes. Lazarus does not lie with his sores exposed on our threshold; he is put out of sight as an uncomely object, and we overlook him. Now and then some uncomfortable political outbreak, now and then some horrible newspaper revelation, some exposure of the condition of a casual workhouse ward, some disclosure of a mingled tangle of sin and crime, wakes us up out of our fool's Paradise only that we may sink back into our sleep again. My brethren, they whose daily calling sends them into the dwellings and to the bedsides of the lowest of the poor, can tell you something of the unequal distribution of the boasted riches of this land.

Nay, you have but to penetrate for yourselves into one of the courts or alleys of this city of yours, to find such pictures ready painted to the life. The contrast between the young Oxford spendthrift and the miserable need of some of the Oxford poor, is a contrast not to be set aside ; nay, to be thought over, dwelt upon, turned to its account, until we learn to ask ourselves the question that will be put to each in the great account, " What hast thou gained with thy treasure in its occu- " pation ?"

And what is the answer? " What hast thou gained ?" What sense have you had of your responsibilities in the sight of Almighty God in their behalf? Have you tried to live as one to whom, as to a steward, has been committed this mighty gift of money, the most powerful agent among natural gifts for good or for evil? What more utterly selfish in this earth really, than the careless recklessness which passes for goodnature, and a generous heart and a liberal hand ? Miserable misnomers! darkness for light and light for darkness, bitter for sweet and sweet for bitter. Grievous as is waste of God's gifts, we must deplore all around us in this place, far more deplorable the effect upon the unfortunate man's own being and character. As touching others, there is indeed loss, but as touching himself, he is preparing against the day of repentance that which will " eat his " flesh as it were with fire." When God gives him the grace of recollection, the bitterness of regret is indeed terrible. To such come home the words of the Hebrew prophets to the self-indulgent of their day : " Tremble, " ye women that are at ease [c];" " Woe to them that are " at ease in Zion [d]."

And all this brings us to the simple rules for our Lenten self-examination, for to such self-knowledge should all Lenten preaching lead. Under the head of the eighth commandment let us ask ourselves two questions: First, have we robbed God? Secondly, have

[c] Isa. xxxii. 11.   [d] Amos vi. 1.

we misused His gifts on ourselves? The two questions
really become one. Under the eighth commandment
they naturally come, according to the words of the
Prophet: "Will a man rob God? Yet ye have robbed
" Me. But ye say, Wherein have we robbed Thee? In
" tithes and offerings ᵉ." Have we counted ourselves
stewards? and what is our account of our stewardship?
Thus, have we spent upon our pleasures, our indulgences,
our softer sins, that which was not meet? Have we
withheld from His poor that which was their due? My
brethren, put not the question from you because your
stewardship may be small, for it is the small stewardship, well husbanded, that yields the richest and most
blessed increase.

To the thoughtful mind the various contrasts between
the wealth and the poverty of our English land is
a very portent. A popular writer of our day has not
shrunk from saying that gold has polluted and cor-
rupted every political community, every social influence,
every family tie, wherever it has come. As Christians,
we shall count such a statement not merely exaggerated,
but heretical. Wealth is the gift of God; to replenish
and subdue the earth is His command. And a gift
rightly used is blessed to the possessor just in proportion to the difficulty of using it aright. For ourselves
we may each in his own place and sphere learn to turn
this dross of earth into precious blessing; to minister
of our temporal substance to the spiritual and bodily
necessities of those who are our brethren; to anticipate
the true riches of the kingdom by a faithful stewardship
of the unrighteous mammon, so that when we " fail
" they may receive us into everlasting habitations."

• Mal. iii. 8.

SERMON VIII.

Personal Responsibility of Man, as to his Influence upon Others.

ST. JOHN i. 40, 41.

"One of the two that heard John speak, was Andrew, Simon
Peter's brother. He first findeth his own brother Simon, and
saith unto him, We have found the Messias, which is, being interpreted, the Christ."

IT has been disputed whether each separate <u>soul</u> be
a fresh creation of God, or derived through generation from the human parent. The former is gene-
rally accepted as the truer view; but the result as to
the influence of the parents on their offspring would
be in either case in effect the same, though varying in
degree. For the soul is influenced by the <u>body</u>, receiving from it impressions and dispositions which impart a character. And thus through the medium of
the body the mental peculiarities of the parent may be
transmitted, and habits or tendencies perpetuated, of
a powerful, though very subtle kind, such as are wit-
nessed by family, and, on a larger scale, by national
distinctions.

This mysterious fact in the history of our race, resting as it does on an universal law of life, exemplifies
very strikingly the consequences of the intimate connexion of man with his fellow-man. What has been
adduced is simply a law of physical influence, but it is

II

founded on moral causes. For as the body influences the soul, so does the soul influence the body. There is a mutual action and re-action, as each impresses the seal of its vital energies on the other, so that in a progressive onward series from generation to generation, the influence of progenitors extends endlessly to their descendants. And thus a very solemn responsibility is established, types of character being reproduced as the consequence of moral states and actions in the forefathers of past ages; and what men are, or do, or make themselves to be, determine, at least in some measure, the natural dispositions of their successors to be created even in far-distant ages, according to laws altogether beyond their power to control. Such moral influences tell everywhere on society, through links which bind closely in one its manifold component members.

We may herein discern the causes of the keen interest which even men of advanced age take in the interests of this present life, and this often equally with their younger cotemporaries. Great social changes, fresh political combinations, the acts of public men,—are matters which excite eager discussion and anxious questioning, even when the immediate concerns of the present time are necessarily of little account in themselves. It is because of the immense influence upon character which such events produce, that such interest is felt. But for this it would be idle to expend upon politics all the energy and thought that they invariably excite. They are not mere questions of the day, nor do they merely affect outward and transient things. What is the secret motive which is now arousing to intensest eagerness many of the oldest, the most devout, the most truly philosophical and Christian-hearted men among yourselves in reference to the projected Uni-

versity Tests Bill ? It is the instinctive consciousness
that in the proposed measure far more is at stake than
any mere immediate disciplinary change or relaxation
of rule of teaching, however important such result might
be.   Beyond this are seen the consequences in the future ; the sure irremediable operation of causes affect-
ing the whole character of this place, penetrating everywhere, working on through successive generations to
the end of time, with results most deleterious, as they
believe, to the whole moral, as well as the doctrinal,
life of this centre of Church education.   As the pressure of air and water tells equally in all directions, so
movements in the social and political world work on
all sides with a like pressure, raising or lowering the
general character, and, as involved in the life of the
body, the individual character,—the life of each separate soul, its moral and religious state before God, its
form and tone, the essence of its moral life, equally as
its outward development ; and this not in time merely,
but through endless ages.

The circumstances and forms of our social laws and
Parliamentary enactments will necessarily pass away,
as all outward things, as at length heaven and earth
will pass away,—but not so their influence.   They will
be found to have left their impression stamped for ever
and ever on the eternal condition of countless souls.
We might well be ashamed of the heat of our political
conflicts, if it were not for the instinctive conviction
that through the fine and subtle organization, connect-
ing the whole intellectual and moral framework of humanity with its social order, every movement is felt
in infinite pulsations indefinitely around and onward,
through ever-widening circles of human life, with consequences to which we can fix no limit.   If we take into

view the moral effects of social and political movements, it is no exaggeration to say that every moment we are legislating for eternity, and shaping the everlasting destiny of souls by our social arrangements.

How remarkable, moreover, it is that these vast currents of secret influence ordinarily gather themselves up into individual centres, and through them are conveyed to the world. A single man is from time to time raised up to reanimate and mould an age. The influence of ages past has already acted to form his character and aims, and then his genius re-acts upon the world around him to stamp on it the enduring impressions to which he had already yielded himself. You may tell the history of our race by the history of the leading men of their time. Life thus ever acts and re-acts. The countless influences of ten thousand times ten thousand individuals concentrate themselves on the separate heroes of successive ages ; as, again, their single influences tell on the generations after generations that follow them. Thus human life, as a whole, progresses and develops, not by decrees of almighty power, not by the will of rulers, not by any fixed laws, but, under the ceaseless guidance of God, by these fine multitudinous influences, in which each man bears his part, influenced and influencing in turn.

Could we penetrate the secrets of the divine order of creation, we should doubtless see that this chain of many links, this wonderful mutual system of influences, lies at the very root of the primary idea of human society as God willed it to be, not merely in special instances, but as an universal law. We are made to live as many members, yet in one body, and these ceaseless endless influences are the links and bands which, having perpetual nourishment ministered to them, and knit together, form and grow into the one living whole of the ever-fluent mass of human life.

The same law extends to the highest order of humanity equally as to the inferior orders. Pre-eminently is this the case in forming Christ's kingdom. Our Lord Himself is above all influences, nothing external to Himself acting in the formation of His character, except according to His own will. He is the one only independent self-originating Man, for His Manhood was formed under the influence of the Godhead, and Himself is God. Under the influence of His Father's will, He willed His Humanity to grow and develop to His full glory. But He owed nothing to mere human influence. He was separate from His brethren in this, that nothing from without influenced Him, but what He Himself willed. The spiritual life of His elect, on the other hand, is the result of manifold varied and combined influences, equally as the same law applies to all other minor forms of man's nature; the will of God, whether directly or indirectly, working through them according to the secret guidance of His Spirit.

How wonderful in this respect was the first opening of Christianity on the world! The first chapter of St. John commences with the eternal generation of Christ; it closes with the history of the personal influences of man on man in forming the nucleus of His Church. Our Lord is described standing alone, as He first unfolds the purpose of His coming to the world. The whole future Church then lived in His individual person. In His loins, as He stood on the banks of the Jordan, already existed in its multitudinous germs the vast communion of the saints to be born in due time. But quickly that wondrous mystical life begins to develop! And this not by any outward manifestation of

power, not by miracle, not by any distinct effort, not by
laboured discourse, but through a secret, silent personal
intercourse.

How touchingly, beautifully simple, were the first
drawings of the Spirit of God! " The next day after
John stood, and two of his disciples ; and looking upon
Jesus as He walked, he saith, Behold the Lamb of God !
And the two disciples heard him speak, and they
followed Jesus.   Then Jesus turned, and saw them following, and saith unto them, What seek ye ?   They
said unto Him, Rabbi, where dwellest Thou ?   He saith
unto them, Come and see.   They came and saw where
He dwelt, and abode with Him that day.   One of the
two which heard John speak, was Andrew, Simon Peter's
brother.   He first findeth his own brother Simon, and
saith unto him, We have found the Messias, which is,
being interpreted, the Christ.   And he brought him to
Jesus. . . . . The day following Jesus would go forth into
Galilee, and findeth Philip, and saith unto him, Follow
Me. . . . Philip findeth Nathanael, and saith unto him,
We have found Him, of whom Moses in the Law, and
the Prophets, did write, Jesus of Nazareth, the son of
Joseph[a]."   Such was the foundation of the Church of
God, the city of the living God.   The full expression
of the truth followed afterwards.   St. Peter's confession, " Thou art the Christ, the Son of the living God,"
was made subsequently to this first ingathering of disciples.   The great promise, " Upon this rock I will
build My Church," was as yet in the future, an after-
power put forth to consolidate what had been begun.
But these personal influences, first of Jesus on Andrew, then of Andrew on Peter ; again of Jesus on
Philip, and then of Philip on Nathanael, were the be-

[a] St. John i. 35—45.

ginning of the conversion of the world; the turning-point of that tremendous revolution in which the history of four thousand years closed, and the modern world of Christianity, and in it the restoration of fallen man, and as a minor result, all true civilization, commenced.

The completion of this new society is but the perfect carrying out of the same law of mutual influences of personal fellowship, in which each individual acts on another, and all in God. The same St. John thus describes the message which was given to him to declare of the glory of the future: "This is the message which we have heard of Him, and declare unto you, that God is light, and in Him is no darkness at all [b]." And then he reveals the preparation within that light of the mystical Bride, the chosen company in intimate association with each other in the same light with God, acting and re-acting on each other in God: "But if we walk in the light, as He is in the light, we have fellowship one with another [c]." The Apostle contemplates the Church of the sanctified walking together within the radiance of a common glory, which he sees streaming from the Presence of God, and which assimilates all in God. The fair supernatural procession passes before his gifted eyes, and within the glory that envelopes the whole body each individual form is luminous with a brightness that reflects itself on others. They know, they exercise their brotherhood; they mutually impart and receive the effects of their mystic fellowship in the gathering together of the energies of a common life, which circulates throughout the enchanted host, to find its rest, from whence it drew its origin, in God. They have lived together influencing each other on

[b] 1 St. John i. 5.   [c] Ibid. i. 7.

earth; they are bound together in a perfected fellowship in the Source, the Fountain-head of their blessed
life, in heaven.

This truth is surely still more momentous if we consider how the verse closes. Holy Scripture makes our
chief hope dependent on this fellowship, for the words
which follow are; "And the Blood of Jesus Christ His
Son cleanseth us from all sin[d]." The connexion is most
vital. "We have fellowship one with another, *and*
the Blood of Jesus Christ cleanseth, &c." The structure of the sentence implies that the precious Blood
flows not around isolated centres, but through the
links of connected chains, in community, not in soli-
tariness, and its power made dependent on this intercommunion. What is this but a repetition in the
world of spirit, of what we have seen to be the universal law both in man's physical and moral being,
that the law of grace is a law of mutual personal influences? It is simply the Same God causing the same
principle on which He had founded nature, to be also
the principle of the operations of eternal life.

It follows that we cannot abdicate our responsibility
in doing our part to diffuse a holy influence without
paralyzing to some extent, at least, the course of grace,
and checking the flow of the precious Blood. What
must our doom be, if we are guilty of spreading posi-
tively an evil influence, poisoning the channels through
which the blessed Spirit yearns to communicate the life
of Christ!

To this subject belongs the whole question of example. Independently of any definite act, or conscious
effort, or studied expression; distinct from any outward circumstance, or power, or gift of genius, this

[d] 1 St. John i. 7.

mysterious influence acts.   Often, when most unob-
trusive, it possesses the greater weight.   Often, too, it
is felt less in the present than in the future.   Long after
words have been forgotten, and deeds have faded into
indistinctness, living only as a dream-like vision on the
memory, the force of example may be insensibly working as fresh, as persuasive as ever.   An example may
haunt us, when the form, and face, and actions of the
man who gave it, have passed from our consciousness.
A consistent unpretending example once set before our
mind, at home, or school, or college, perhaps at the time
the subject of jest, or at best but lightly regarded, rises
up in after years as a witness for God, and a condemnation to oneself, moved to confess the sins of early years.

This same influence manifestly extends into the
highest regions of life.   It is the explanation which
Holy Scripture gives of the perfect moulding of the
character of the Humanity of Jesus.   Speaking of our
Lord, it says, "The Son can do nothing of Himself,
but what He seeth the Father do."   While our Lord
owed nothing to His fellow-man, He nevertheless received ceaseless impressions, as man from man, so He
from His Father in heaven.   It is the perfection of the
law of example in the most transcendent order of created
existence.   A type ever before the mind, and acting
upon it to form it after itself, is what we understand
as an example, and precisely this the eternal Father
was to our Lord.   And that this is the law of all
heavenly life seems to be most probable.   The angels,
apparently, are what they are because they always "behold the face of" their "Father which is in heaven."
They see in God the divine idea which they were intended to embody, and their life grows to be a perpetual unchanging expression of it.   The final develop-

ment of redeemed humanity, the complete conversion of souls restored to the image of God within the mystical Body of Christ, depends on this same law; for it was revealed to St. John, that, "We shall be like Him, for we shall see Him as He is." The final transformation of the faithful will be the result of the vision of the perfect type, the example of the perfect Manhood, which is one with God. So mysterious is this power of example, that we are wholly unconscious while it operates on us. Its very imperceptibleness is one great cause of its irresistible force. It is proverbial how tricks are insensibly caught, how quickly the gait and tone of voice take the shape, or accent, which is constantly presented to us. And what we see so unmistakeably manifested in ordinary outward habits, equally prevails in man's hidden life. The soul is indeed more sensitive of such impressions than the body, and much of the good and evil around us arises, not from direct teaching, nor from personal effort, nor altogether from the inworking power of God, but from this silent mysterious agency which it has pleased God to cause to be exercised by man upon his fellow-man.

And what an awful idea attaches to human acts and words, if we trace the operation of this principle. The ruin or the saving of others hangs on what, when in actual operation, we cannot control, although the influence originally emanated from ourselves, is the reproduction of what we ourselves have been.

Nor is there any limit to this influence. Far beyond the possible reach of our words or acts, without intercourse or mutual knowledge, the secret power of what we have been or are, may tell, and continue to work out its consequences, when acts and words are lost in the shadows of a long-forgotten past.

There is no distinct text telling us that we shall reap
the fruit of these effects of our own life on others.
Scripture needs not reveal what conscience sufficiently
declares. We bear in ourselves a witness to our responsibility for the consequences of our example on others.
What an intense aggravation of the sorrows of Adam
and Eve must it have been, to see their offspring copy
their acts, to feel the terrible doom, far worse than the
curse within themselves, that in giving life, they must
give birth to plastic forms which age after age would
receive and exhibit the impression of their own sins,
generation after generation perpetuating the consequences of their corruption. Even the heathen felt
the intensity of the guilt of an evil example set heed-
lessly, when they left on record the momentous warning
that "maxima debetur pueris reverentia." They could
see the misery of the pollution transmitted even unconsciously by the practised sinner to the unwary suscepti-
bility of youth.

The awful guilt of this side of human conduct is the
more to be dreaded, because we can never gather up
these items of ever-developing effects of evil. We may,
in searching into our past life, count up its evil deeds,
and sinful words, and positive omissions, with compara-
tive accuracy. But can we by any sifting of our conscience, by the most earnest desire to cleanse away past
sin by timely confession, recall, or possibly estimate the
evil that we have wrought, and may be still working, by
a bad example? After all our closest self-examinations
we are constrained to pass by, as beyond the possible
reach of memory, many items in the catalogue even of
actual transgressions. But we can never even attempt
to guess at the amount or extent of the consequences

of an evil influence upon others, though distinctly trace-
able in the eye of God to ourselves. The repentant
infidel author may buy up the unsold copies of his
writings; the converted thief may compensate the
injury over which he mourns by the restoration of
the stolen goods; the defamer of his brethren may
publicly acknowledge his false accusations. Acts may
be repaired by acts, words by words. But no repara-
tion can extend to the influence of an evil example.
You cannot track its path, or if you could, the evil can
be undone only by the repentance of him who has
suffered from it, not of him that wrought it. It has
entered into another's life, and thus has passed beyond
one's own power. The truest penitent may live to see
the agonies of the lost soul which traces the beginning
of its sinful course to the bad example which he had
set; himself saved, his work of evil in another's soul
sealed to a hopeless condemnation.

We can therefore form no adequate conception of life
and its awful issues, if we regard the effect of our conduct only in reference to ourselves. This view presents
but one side of our responsibility. We may not indeed
deliberately design the exercise of our powers in pro-
ducing influences on others; we may not be conscious
of such powers. As we may possess gifts of genius or
virtue, and exercise them, not dwelling on them, not
realizing them, and yet are responsible for their use, so
likewise with regard to this mysterious power of influence. Nor think that it is only the great and gifted
which can exercise this power. Not merely is it an universal law of life, necessarily accompanying all human
actions; but the least may influence the greatest. It
was St. Andrew, that influenced St. Peter to "come and

see" Jesus. One least spoken of among the Apostles
influenced the one who took the foremost place among
them, as if to shew that such power is independent of
personal superiority. Again, the latest Apostle, St.
Paul, is employed by God to correct St. Peter, even as
to his inspired teaching.

·The honours of life fall to the lot of the great and the
gifted. The race of fame is to the swift. But the very
feeblest in a family, in a college, or religious community,
may raise the tone and purify the spiritual life of the
whole body, even as, alas! on the other hand, the abuse
of this power may in any one degrade the character,
and defile the conscience of all the other members.
But a yet greater evil lies in an insensibility, a heed-
lessness to the power of this influence. There is hope
for the agent of an unholy influence, so long as he is
conscious of the power that he wields. As God hates
and casts far from Him the lukewarm, as worse than
what is either hot or cold, so one dead to the consciousness of spiritual powers and responsibilities towards
others' lives, is the more hopelessly reprobate. There is
hope so long as the sense of the evil communicated to
others makes one sensitive to the evil which exists in
oneself. The sight of ruin wrought by one's own evil
agency, may awaken the conscience to the deadly
power which sin exerts. But if to being a murderer of
another's life we add the utter disregard of such consequences of our acts, where is the possibility of remorse?
In the cold recklessness of the thought, "Am I my
brother's keeper," one has all the more fatally closed
the door against the hope of a return to God. The
sight of one's own sin, in the loss of another's purity, is
one of the influences which God has mercifully willed

to be the awakening of the slumbering conscience. If oneself is guilty of having caused that sin, or of having failed to remedy it when the opportunity offered, the sight of evil in another, as one's own work, is the most powerful reflection of one's own character. To be dead to such an influence is to be twice dead, as, on the other hand, to be conscious of one's power for good is to raise oneself to a higher level of spiritual life. To care for another's soul is to rise in one's estimate of one's own. We rise in raising others, even as we are raised in their rising. Thus men act and re-act on each other unceasingly. Human society was intended by God to be the sphere wherein each individual member might strive with another in the manifestation of His grace, as a means of furthering His own glory; and blessed is the lot of any one, however lowly, however feeble, who, standing it may be alone, abides stedfast in his own heart, bearing witness for the truth and sanctity of the law of his God; and thus becomes in the midst of his brethren the centre of an ever-widening influence of a pure and holy conversation.

Before closing, a few practical suggestions may be added.

1. Recognise the many links which bind one man to another as a distinct purpose of God, fulfilling a material part of our probation,—not a constraint hampering our independence and thwarting our will, but a ceaseless discipline of the utmost moment, counteracting the fatal selfishness of our nature.

2. Consider how much we owe to the example of others. Call up from the past the manifold forms of influence exerted by a parent, a sister, a brother, a friend, it may be a dependant, one, it may be, least

honoured among men. Think of the recompense of
everlasting honour which that teaching, that living witness for God, may be now inheriting.

3. Weigh the consequences of all expressions, whether
in word or deed, which take their outward shape from
your inner life; feel how they live and work on, ex-
tending themselves, it may be, far and wide. A single
word boldly spoken for God, even a silence that has
reproved some miserable boast; a suggestion; a hint;
a high principle firmly asserted, may be, in its eventual
consequences, the saving of many souls; may commence a revolution in the society in which you move,
even as, on the contrary, an evil witness will bear its
fruit, to rise up against him who bore it, before the
judgment-seat of God.

4. We are all taking our parts in the battle-field, in
which Satan is ever striving against God, and each one
of us is either leagued with the Evil one, and furthering
the ruin of his many victims, or, united with Christ, is
becoming more and more in his daily conversation
a saviour, a healer of the degradation and pollution
"which is in the world through lust."

5. Yet let not your left hand know what your right
hand doeth. Guard all the while the yet greater grace
on which thy own inward life hangs, the grace of lowli-
ness and self-forgetting love. Self does not become
more prominent as we enter into the life of others,
rather it is more and more lost as the spirit of self-
sacrifice extends. To be oneself hidden, is really to
promote the truest influence, as leaven works secretly
in the meal. Our Lord emptied Himself, as He entered
into the life of humanity, and "took upon Him the form
of a servant, and became obedient unto death, even the

death of the cross ;" and yet, in making Himself "of no
reputation," He restored the lost world. So dying in
Him, we live. So living no longer to ourselves, but to
Him who loved us, and gave Himself for us, we pass
into the higher fellowship with all who in God are daily
more and more becoming lost to themselves, that they
may possess His fulness, and share His perfect joy.

SERMON IX.

𝔓ersonal 𝔚esponsibility of 𝔐an, in the 𝔊reat 𝔄ccount.

HEBREWS ix. 27.

" To die,—but after this the judgment."

STEP by step, in the course of sermons now drawing to a close, we have seen the responsibility of man developed, expanded, growing and accumulating before our eyes. We have seen it enforced on this side and on that; in all a man's relations, in all his privileges, in every gift, in every opportunity of using a gift. Every relation creates a duty; every gift requires that we put it to use. It were enough to say that God has revealed to us that He will require us to give account for all. But we may go further back than this. Man's gift of reason, which makes responsibility possible, makes it also inevitable. He may brutify himself: but even thus he cannot become as a brute unknowing of good or evil; for he has chosen the evil and refused the good. He may deface the image in which he was created; but he cannot unmake himself. He may live the grovelling life of the beasts; but he cannot share their innocent unconsciousness. For that which he was made, he is responsible to Him who made him.

And when we pass from those who, even among

I

the heathen, are without excuse, to those, in comparison of whom they may seem almost free from responsibility, we see that the Christian cannot be as the mere heathen.   Christ has died *for all;*—but *to us* He has been made known, in His person, in His love, in His work, in His sacrifice.   In His Incarnation He lays hold on us; on His Cross He stretches out His arms to us; in His Descent and His Ascension He fills all things, He embraces all things; He leads His captivity captive; He receives gifts for men in recognition of universal sovereignty; He gives gifts to men for the perfecting of the saints.   For the knowledge of the revelation, for the mercy of the redemption, man is responsible to Him in whose person the mystery of the ages was revealed, in whose blood the atoning sacrifice for the sins of the world was accomplished.

Yet more.   There is One who came to be with us when our Redeemer was withdrawn; a Presence so precious that it was expedient for us that Christ should go away; a Being so awful that the very atonement of Christ is no atonement for sin against Him.   He is with us, He is among us; nay, He is within us; the Spirit, who is the Life of the Church, distributing severally His gifts and graces, ordinary or sacramental, as He will; the Spirit, whose Divine Presence in our spirits makes us temples of an in-dwelling God; the Spirit, who is given to every man to profit withal.   For every spiritual grace man is responsible to the Spirit, whose kingdom the Church is, whose temples we are. And "if any man defile the temple of God, him shall God destroy."

To the Father who created us, to the Son who redeemed us, to the Holy Ghost who dwelleth in us, we have to give account, not merely by the enactment of

a positive law, but by the declaration of an eternal
necessity, which forbids the divorce of responsibility
from the consciousness of privilege and power. And
this is ours, not as being atoms merged in the corporate
existence and workings of the Church, drops in the
great sea that welters round the steps of the Throne,
but as presented individually to Him with whom we
have to do; brought face to face with Him at every
turn of life ; either consciously walking with Him, like
the Prophet of the patriarchal world, or less consciously
(through a blindness self-incurred), but no less really
accompanied and watched by a Divine Presence which
we only recognise when it thwarts us, like the angel
whom Balaam had not at first his eyes open to see.

Again, there is a general way of recognising all
this, which easily admits it, but with little fruit. But
we further trace the lesson into its details ; and we
have to confess ourselves accountable for the possession and the use of every one of those separate gifts
which form or adorn the master of this world and heir
of the next :—

Whether it be *intellect*,—given us to comprehend, in
a measure, that which passes comprehension in the deep
things of God,—in His manifested works, in His revealed ways in Christ; to touch, as it were, on the
confines of spiritual things, and to receive the commu-
nications, the inspirations, the infused graces of God's
Holy Spirit ;—yet intellect, when unsanctified, the
special and characteristic attribute of the enemy of
God :—

Or *speech*,—our glory, the best member that we have,
when consecrated to the praises of God and to the proclamation of His will ;—yet in its misuse a fire, a world
of iniquity, defiling the whole body, setting on fire the

course of nature, itself set on fire of hell ; made to bless
God, used to curse men :—

Or *time,*—the stuff that our lives are made of, the
seed-field in which we are permitted to sow for eternity ;
time, which is given us for work, given us for thought,
given us for prayer ; given to carry us on from strength
to strength till we appear before the God of gods in
Sion ;—but wasted, it may be, or rather (for there is no
such thing as mere waste of time) abused in vanities
and pleasures which perish in the using, in raking together stones for the tomb of our sepulture, or fagots
for the fire that is to burn us.   There are two Latin
sayings* which give the two portraits of our days : " Good
every one, but the best kept to the last :"—this as they
come from God.   " Each one woundeth, the last slay-
eth :"—this, as the serpent's tooth has poisoned them :—

Or *money,*—the most hazardous, yet not the less the
real gift of God ; given to us to make friends, eternal
friends, with the mammon of unrighteousness :—and yet,
after all, the unrighteous mammon still, which men are
minded to serve, either with God (but this they cannot
do), or without Him ; so that it is hard for the rich man
to enter into the kingdom of heaven.   It may open
heaven to us if we have sent our treasure there before
us.   But oh! how much oftener it is clutched and carried with us on the downward road, as if we had a toll
to pay to open the gates of hell !

And as all these gifts, and the many others which
might be instanced, go to mould a man's character, to
give it its form and pressure, ay, go to mould the characters of others by the imperceptible, irresistible inter-
dependence of society, for these things too we are re-

---

* 1. " Multos felices, ultimum felicissimum."
   2. " Vulnerant omnes, enecat ultima."

sponsible ; for that which we have made ourselves, for
that which we have made others. We have a burden
to bear for one another ; and yet every man must bear
his own burden. We are our brethren's keepers, though
no man can redeem his brother's soul.

But in this multifarious responsibility there is necessarily something of vagueness and uncertainty. One
by one we have realised the details ; and each has stood
out clearly and distinctly, written as in letters of fire
on the dark curtain of our nightly communings. One
by one the burdens upon us have seemed more than
we could bear. But what is their cumulative effect?

It is, perhaps, bewilderment. Take the colours on
a painter's palette, as they lie side by side so brilliant
in their beauty. Try the experiment of blending them
into one, and what will be the result? One undistin-
guishable blotch of mud ! And so it may prove to be
with the mind, overstrained in the attempt to grasp
the total of that which has been so alarming in its
details.

Or the result may be carelessness. The first impression may have been deep, the second slighter, the third
slighter still ; and before the catalogue has been gone
through, attention flags ; some new trick of the tempter's
art dazzles the eyes ; and the man turns again, forgetting
the burden on his back, to chase the butterflies of his
childhood.

Or it may be desperation ;—and like a beast of chase
that faces round and breaks away through the array of
its pursuers, he may altogether break the yoke and
burst the bonds.

And thus life glides away ; and while responsibility is
accumulating, the sense of it grows dull and dead ; conscience loses its sensitiveness and power, becomes cal-

lous, is scared as with a hot iron. " Let us eat and drink, for to-morrow we die," the man chooses for his text,—not going on to " Be not deceived,"—absolutely deaf to " Awake to righteousness." So he may live, so he may die. Shocking as the thought is, it is possible ; nay, when we look outwards on the world, when we look deep into our own hearts, can we deny that it is easy ; can we deny that it is, in the strictest sense of the word, natural ?

But if a man can live, if a man can die with his eyes shut or his heart hardened to the sense of his responsibility, is he therefore free ? If this were all, if death were the end of all, then those who were content to accept the life and the death of the brute,—"Let us eat and drink, for to-morrow we die,"—might be almost deemed impregnable in their position. Fallen so low, it might seem that they could fall no further. But though there are instances of this kind, how is it that they are so rare, even among those whose interest it would seem not to believe ? How is it that conscience does make herself heard in the closing hours of life, when she has been bound and tongue-tied before ? It is because at the approach of death there is something lifted of the veil that shrouds the unseen. Then the voice of warning assumes the tone of prophecy ; and the message is, " It is appointed to all men once to die, and after this the judgment."

Then, at last, all masks drop off, all veils fall away. It will be of little advantage to have silenced conscience, in the day when her whispers are replaced by the record written in the opened books. It will be no time to plead ignorance or lack of memory, when the light of the Judge's countenance shall illuminate the secret chambers of all hearts. The power will fail to brave the will of

God and renounce our allegiance to Him, when a man finds himself face to face with the Everlasting, the All-knowing, the Almighty; within His grasp, subject to His justice; only severed, if severed by the man's own will and acts, from His mercy. Of all the terrors of that day, to men who, while the day of salvation lasted, have refused to be persuaded of the terrors of the Lord, which will be the chief?

Will it be the exposure of all our sins and all our shame; the sins that we might have hidden, might have cleansed in His blood, but would not; the shame that . we might have anticipated by taking shame to ourselves, clothing ourselves in our own confusion before Him, that we might receive from Him robes of grace and glory? This would be sufficiently terrible. Think, but for a moment, what an influence this sense of exposure to your fellow-sinners' judgment exerts over you even now. Ask yourselves, Has it never happened that you have felt quite calm and comfortable under the secret consciousness of an action, which has caused you agony as soon as you began to think that your brethren and neighbours knew it as well as yourselves? Is not this the plain and simple history of nine-tenths of the cases of desperate suicide that we hear of? Is it not that a man who has borne stoutly the knowledge of his own wrong-doing, plunges anywhere, into the darkness of the abyss, rather than face the judgment, the contempt, the triumph, the mockery of his fellow-men? And yet this might prove to be no more than a nine days' wonder in a narrow neighbourhood, if he could take courage to face it; and he might live through it, and wait to lift up his head again, when it was over. But in that day all will be naked before all the world; no shelter in the present, no hope in the future!

But amidst that great company—the first and last gathering of the universal human race—there are individuals whose presence may suggest a special pang. There are those whom we have known only too well, those whose companions we have been in vanity or in sin, those for whom we have to answer. If we have led souls into sin, either to share our own wickedness or to follow it ; if we have made them the victims of our vile passions, or have taught them to indulge their own ; if our words have shaken their faith, or hardened them in ungodliness ; if our recklessness, real or assumed, has confirmed them in evil courses which they were hesitating to follow ; nay, if our silence has left them unwarned and unreproved, when a word spoken in season might have saved them from sin ; then indeed the burden of responsibility will be as lead upon our souls in that day, when not Cain himself will venture to say a second time, " Am I my brother's keeper ?"

Again : there will be those there who had a responsibility for us, and who knew it, and did their best to discharge it ; those who loved us, and watched over us in our childhood ; those who lay in our bosoms, and would have won us by their gentle influence from the rebelliousness of our maturer age ; those who have tended and nursed us in our decline. Their Christian love cannot lack its reward for themselves. But if all this, their ministry, their affection, their devotion, has been without avail to us, with what feelings are we to meet their eyes in that day ? Say, then, which will be the deepest shame, the keenest agony, to look on those whom we have dragged down to hell, or on those who would, had we not refused, have led us upward to heaven ;—on those who heap upon us the curses of their own perdition, or on those who, it may be,

are feeling for us the last grief that they shall ever
know,—

> " pitifully fixing
> Tender reproaches, insupportable."

But we are still lingering in the outskirts and suburbs
of that judgment-place ; as if for very shame and fear
turning our eyes and thoughts away from the throne
and Him that sitteth thereon. But though the presence
of the universal race of Adam in that day shall en-
hance its horrors for the wicked, it is not to them, or
any of them, that we are responsible ; it is not they that
shall fix our doom. And even that which has seemed
most terrible has no terror in this respect, by reason of
the terror that exceedeth,—the terror of the Lord, the
great white throne and Him that sitteth on it, from
whose face the earth and the heavens flee away. But
herein lies the defect of our limited minds. We can to
some extent grasp those adjuncts and circumstances of
terror. But that on which they all attend, that which
gives their nature and their potency to them all, is in
itself indescribable, unutterable, inconceivable. We can
but climb step by step the height of mortal agony ; and
then discover that we are still as far as ever from real-
ising that which lies beyond. But it is in this mere
and sheer blank, a blank which we know is in our own
finite natures, that we recognise an awfulness that we
cannot measure, a vision of judgment before which all
that we have conceived as most appalling, utterly disappears ; and we stand solitary, ay, in the presence of
angels and fiends and men we stand solitary, in our sins
before the throne. No trees of the garden will be there
to shelter us ; no rocks and mountains to cover us, when
we are brought up from the darkness and shadow of
death, to feel beating upon us, as if it were concentrated

on us alone, the insufferable brightness of the revelation of God.

And not of God only, but of Him who is God and
Man,—of the man Christ Jesus, to whom the Father has
committed this judgment, even because He is the Son
of Man.   And this is a thought which suggests a further
question, a question which will demand an answer when
we commune with our own hearts.   Is it a comfort to
us, or is it not, to know that He, who shall sit on that
throne judging right, is the same Christ who in the form
of man lived and suffered and died for us?

There are passages in the Word of Inspiration which
speak of this as anything rather than a comfort.   There
we read, that "Every eye shall see Him, and they also
which pierced Him ; and all the kindreds of the earth
shall wail because of Him."   There we read, "Of how
much sorer punishment shall he be thought worthy,
who hath trodden under foot the Son of God, and hath
counted the blood of the covenant, wherewith he was
sanctified, an unholy thing, and hath done despite unto
the Spirit of Grace :—for we know Him that hath said,
Vengeance belongeth unto Me, I will recompense, saith
the Lord : . . . It is a fearful thing to fall into the hands
of the living God."

These, and the many statements of the like sort which
God's Word contains, do but bring the general principle,
that all responsibility is proportioned to the knowledge
of duty and to the mercies which we have received, into
clearer light, by applying it to the one case which trans-
cends all others—the knowledge of Christ as a revelation, and the gift of Christ as a propitiation :—not the
knowledge only, or even chiefly, though this is the
greatest thing conceivable, save one ; but, in addition,
that one, *the gift* of Christ ; the love of the Father who

spared not His Only-begotten Son ; the love of the Son dying for mankind ; and those scalding tears which fell upon Jerusalem, in token that the things that belonged to her peace were finally and for ever hidden from her eyes.

These are the considerations which lead up to that most simple, most awful expression of the woe to come, —" *the wrath of the Lamb.*"

But in the mercy of God there is another side to this. That which makes the idea of the Lamb's wrath so terrible is, that it contradicts nature. It was not for this, it was not to punish the sins of the world that He was manifested, but to take away the sins of the world, to bear them in His own person. There may be,—indeed there will be, those on whom that wrath must come to the uttermost ; but it were blasphemy to say, that for this He came into the world :—it were but little short of blasphemy to say, that the purpose for which He came into the world will fail : and " God sent not His Son into the world to condemn the world ; but that the world through Him might be saved." And when we hear that He has this judgment committed to Him, even because He is the Son of Man, is not the significance of this the same ? Are we to suppose that the Son of Man is set to judge, that the sons of men may be condemned ? In those courts of justice which are the most august of earthly scenes in proportion as they present some faint image of God's eternal attribute, we are not tempted to think that trial by our peers is a precaution of despotism or a device of cruelty. And will it be a hardship to those who stand before yonder judgment-seat, that a human nature is united with the Divine in our Redeemer-Judge ; a nature which can thrill with the pulsations of our hearts ; through which He knows the power of temptations, though they had no power over Him; and can sympathise with weakness to which He never yielded?

Brethren, it is given to us, each and all, through the mercy of God, and by the help of His gracious Spirit, to decide whether this compassion, this sympathy, this brotherly love, shall have free course and be glorified in us. If we plead *Not Guilty*, and stand stoutly on our merits and our rights, what are they,—what are we, —and what must our judgment be? We must plead *Guilty*, that His loving-kindness may have its way. We must plead and cry for the mercy which is our only hope.

In kingdoms of this world, the sovereign entrusts the administration of justice to others, and reserves the crowning grace of mercy to himself. But on that day there is One Judgment-seat, Mercy-seat: there is One that sitteth, our Judge, our King, our merciful Lord and Saviour. He is there to condemn and execute judgment :—but He is there also to pardon and receive into glory. Oh, righteous Judge! oh, merciful Saviour! give us that first grace, to seek and strive for more; to agree with our adversary quickly, while we are in the way with him; to hear the voice of tenderness uttering the message which the Prophets bore to Israel, "Why will ye die? I have no pleasure in the death of him that dieth, saith the Lord!" If we look to Him on the Cross, and see Him suffering not the bodily agonies of that precious death, the penalty of our sins, alone, but the greater and more abhorrent burden of those sins themselves,—if we can repent of all that we have laid upon Him,—if we can find in our hearts to love Him according to the love wherewith He has loved us,—then that Judgment-seat will, indeed, be a Mercy-seat to us;

then, in the very day of judgment, "mercy shall rejoice against judgment."

Choose ye, dearly beloved brethren, whom the Christ who died for you is coming to judge ! Choose, while His mercy and long-suffering wait,—while His grace is freely yours to enable you to choose the good :—that, "as it is appointed to men once to die, but after this the judgment, so Christ, who was once offered to bear *your* sins, may unto you, and all that look for Him, appear the second time, without sin, unto salvation !"

PRINTED BY JAMES PARKER AND CO., CROWN-YARD, OXFORD.

A List of Books

RECENTLY PUBLISHED BY

JAMES PARKER AND CO.,

OXFORD, AND 377, STRAND, LONDON.

NEW WORKS.

SIR JOHN T. COLERIDGE.:

MEMOIR OF THE REV. J. KEBLE, M.A. By Sir J. T. COLE-RIDGE. *Third Edition.* Post 8vo., cloth, 10s. 6d.

THE LORD BISHOP OF SALISBURY.

THE BAMPTON LECTURES FOR 1868. THE ADMINISTRATION OF THE HOLY SPIRIT IN THE BODY OF CHRIST. By GEORGE MOBERLY, D.C.L., Lord Bishop of Salisbury. *Second Edition.* Crown 8vo. [*In the Press.*

SERMONS ON THE BEATITUDES, with others mostly preached before the University of Oxford; to which is added a Preface relating to the recent volume of "Essays and Reviews." By GEORGE MOBERLY, D.C.L., Lord Bishop of Salisbury. *Third Edition.* Crown 8vo. [*In the Press.*

THE LATE REV. JOHN KEBLE.

MISCELLANEOUS POEMS BY THE REV. JOHN KEBLE, M.A., Vicar of Hursley. [With Preface by G. M.] *Second Edition.* Fcap., cloth, 6s.

THE PSALTER, OR PSALMS OF DAVID: In English Verse. By the Rev. J. KEBLE, M.A. *Fourth Edition.* Fcap. cl., 6s.

LYRA INNOCENTIUM. Thoughts in Verse on Christian Children, their Ways, and their Privileges. By the Rev. J. KEBLE, M.A. *Twelfth Edition.* Fcap. 8vo., 7s. 6d. [*Nearly ready.*

₊ The above three Volumes are printed uniform in size and binding with the Fcap. edition of "The Christian Year." Together they form "The Complete Poetical Works of the late Rev. John Keble." 4 vols., Fcap. 8vo., 27s.

ON EUCHARISTICAL ADORATION. By the Rev. JOHN KEBLE, M.A.—With CONSIDERATIONS SUGGESTED BY A LATE PASTORAL LETTER (1858) ON THE DOCTRINE OF THE MOST HOLY EUCHARIST. *Third Edition.* 8vo., cloth, 6s.—*A Cheap Edition,* 24mo., sewed, 2s.

SERMONS, OCCASIONAL AND PAROCHIAL. By the Rev. JOHN KEBLE, M.A. 8vo., cloth, 12s.

VILLAGE SERMONS ON THE BAPTISMAL SERVICE. By the Rev. JOHN KEBLE, M.A. 8vo., cloth, 5s.

THE FIRST EDITION OF THE CHRISTIAN YEAR, printed in Facsimile. In 2 vols., Fcap., paper boards, as first issued, 7s. 6d.

To this reprint is appended a list containing "all the variations of any importance from the original text which the author made in later editions."

1269(3)10

2   *NEW THEOLOGICAL WORKS, (continued).*

THE LORD BISHOP OF WINCHESTER ELECT.

A CHARGE DELIVERED TO THE DIOCESE OF OXFORD AT
HIS EIGHTH VISITATION, Nov. 11, 1869, by SAMUEL, LORD BISHOP OF OXFORD, Lord High Almoner to Her Majesty the Queen, and Chancellor of the Order of the Garter. 8vo., sewed, 1s. 6d.

ADDRESSES TO THE CANDIDATES FOR ORDINATION ON
THE QUESTIONS IN THE ORDINATION SERVICE. By SAMUEL, LORD BISHOP OF OXFORD, Chancellor of the Most Noble Order of the Garter, and Lord High Almoner to Her Majesty the Queen. *Fifth Thousand.* Crown 8vo., cloth, 6s.

REV. E. B. PUSEY, D.D.

EIRENICON. PART I. THE CHURCH OF ENGLAND A POR-
TION OF CHRIST'S ONE HOLY CATHOLIC CHURCH, AND A MEANS OF RESTORING VISIBLE UNITY. AN EIRENICON, in a Letter to the Author of "The Christian Year." By E. B. PUSEY, D.D., Regius Professor of Hebrew, and Canon of Christ Church. *Sixth Thousand.* 8vo., cloth, 7s. 6d.

EIRENICON. PART II. FIRST LETTER to the Very Rev. J. H.
NEWMAN, D.D., in explanation chiefly in regard to the Reverential Love due to the ever-blessed Theotokos, and the Doctrine of her "Immaculate Conception;" with an Analysis of Cardinal de Turrecremata's work on the "Immaculate Conception." By E. B. PUSEY, D.D. 8vo., cloth, 7s. 6d.

EIRENICON. PART III. IS HEALTHFUL RE-UNION IM-
POSSIBLE? By the Rev. E. B. PUSEY, D.D. 8vo. *[Nearly Ready.*

TRACTATUS DE VERITATE CONCEPTIONIS BEATISSIMÆ
VIRGINIS, pro Facienda Relatione coram Patribus Concilii Basileæ, Anno Domini MCCCXXXVII., Mense Julio. De mandato Sedes Apostolicæ Legatorum, eidem Sacro Concilio præsidentium. Compilatus per Reverendum Patrem, FRATREM JOANNEM DE TURRECREMATA, Sacræ Theologiæ Professorem, Ordinis Prædicatorum, Tunc Sacri Apostolici Palatii Magistrum. Postea Illustrissimum et Reverendissimum S. R. Ecclesiæ Cardinalem, Episcopum Portuensem. Primo impressus Romæ, apud Antonium Bladum, Asulanum, MDXLVII. Small 4to. (850 pp.), cloth, 12s.

ELEVEN ADDRESSES DURING A RETREAT OF THE COM-
PANIONS OF THE LOVE OF JESUS, engaged in Perpetual Intercession for the Conversion of Sinners. By the Rev. E. B. PUSEY, D.D., &c. 8vo., cloth, 3s. 6d.

DANIEL THE PROPHET. Nine Lectures delivered in the Divinity
School of the University of Oxford. With a new Preface. By E. B. PUSEY, D.D., &c. *Third Edition. Fifth Thousand.* 8vo., cloth, 10s. 6d.

THE MINOR PROPHETS; with a Commentary Explanatory and
Practical, and Introductions to the Several Books. By E. B. PUSEY, D.D., &c. 4to., sewed. 5s. each part.

Part I. contains HOSEA—JOEL, INTRODUCTION. | Part III. AMOS vi. 6 to MICAH i. 12.
Part II. JOEL, INTRODUCTION—AMOS vi. 6. | Part IV. *[In the Press.*

THE LORD BISHOP OF BRECHIN.

AN EXPLANATION OF THE THIRTY-NINE ARTICLES.
With an Epistle Dedicatory to the Rev. E. B. PUSEY, D.D. By A. P. FORBES, D.C.L., Bishop of Brechin. Post 8vo., 2 vols., cloth, 19s. 6d.

A SHORT EXPLANATION OF THE NICENE CREED, for the
Use of Persons beginning the Study of Theology. By ALEXANDER PENROSE FORBES, D.C.L., Bishop of Brechin. *Second Edition.* Crown 8vo., cloth, 6s.

EARL NELSON.

FAMILY PRAYERS. By EARL NELSON. With the Psalter and a Calendar of Lessons, for the use of the Master. Limp cloth, 1s. *Third Edit.* The Family Prayers, with Responses and Variations for the Different Seasons, for General Use, may be had separately, in paper covers, at 3d. each; or with the Psalter,' limp cloth, 9d.

Also, the Calendar of Lessons; a Course of Reading for the Christian Year, for Private or Family Use. Limp cloth, 6d.

REV. DR. HANNAH.

HOLLOWNESS, NARROWNESS, AND FEAR: Warnings from the Jewish Church. Three Lectures delivered at Cuddesden Theological College, in Ember-week, Sept., 1869, by J. HANNAH, D.C.L., Warden of Trinity College, Glenalmond. (Published by request.) Crown 8vo., limp cloth, 2s.

REV. CANON GREGORY.

SERMONS ON THE POORER CLASSES OF LONDON, preached before the University of Oxford. By ROBERT GREGORY, M.A., of Corpus Christi College; Canon of St. Paul's, and Vicar of St. Mary the Less, Lambeth. 8vo., cloth, 5s.

HON. AND REV. W. H. LYTTELTON.

FORM OF PRAISE AND PRAYER IN THE MANNER OF OFFICES. Edited by the Hon. and Rev. W. H. LYTTELTON, M.A. Cr. 8vo., 3s. 6d.

REV. CANON WOODFORD.

TRACTS FOR THE CHRISTIAN SEASONS. Third Series. Edited by the Rev. J. R. WOODFORD, M.A., Vicar of Leeds, Examining Chaplain to the Bishop of Oxford. 4 vols. Fcap. 8vo., cloth, 14s.

REV. CANON JENKINS.

THE AGE OF THE MARTYRS; or, the First Three Centuries of the Work of the Church of our Lord and Saviour Jesus Christ. By the Rev. J. D. JENKINS, B.D., Canon of Pieter Maritzburg; Fellow of Jesus College, Oxford. Crown 8vo., cloth, 6s.

REV. G. B. HOWARD.

THE SYRIAN CHRISTIANS OF MALABAR: otherwise called the Christians of S. Thomas. By the Rev. EDAVALIKEL PHILIPOS, Chorepiscopus, Cathanar of the Great Church at Cottayam, in Travancore. Edited by the Rev. G. B. HOWARD, B.A., Chaplain of S. Mary's, Stone, near Dartford. Crown 8vo., limp cloth, 2s. 6d.

REV. W. H. RIDLEY.

THE EVERY-DAY COMPANION. By the Rev. W. H. RIDLEY, M.A., Rector of Hambleden, Bucks. PT. I. Fcap. 8vo., cloth, 2s. PT. II. 1s. 6d. Or in One Volume, cloth, 3s.

REV. WILLIAM BRIGHT, D.D.

A HISTORY OF THE CHURCH, from the EDICT of MILAN, A.D. 313, to the COUNCIL of CHALCEDON, A.D. 451. By WILLIAM BRIGHT, D.D., Regius Professor of Ecclesiastical History and Canon of Christ Church, Oxford. *Second Edition.* Post 8vo., price 10s. 6d.

ANCIENT COLLECTS and OTHER PRAYERS, Selected for Devotional Use from various Rituals, with an Appendix on the Collects in the Prayer-book. By WILLIAM BRIGHT, D.D. *Fourth Edition.* Antique cloth, 5s.; morocco, 8s.; antique calf, 10s. 6d.

REV. R. PAYNE SMITH, D.D.

THE AUTHENTICITY AND MESSIANIC INTERPRETATION OF THE PROPHECIES OF ISAIAH vindicated in a Course of Sermons preached before the University of Oxford, by the Rev. R. PAYNE SMITH, D.D., Canon of Christ Church, Regius Professor of Divinity. 8vo., cloth, 10s. 6d.

ARCHDEACON FREEMAN.

THE PRINCIPLES OF DIVINE SERVICE; or, An Inquiry concerning the True Manner of Understanding and Using the Order for Morning and Evening Prayer, and for the Administration of the Holy Communion in the English Church. By the Ven. ARCHDEACON FREEMAN, M.A., Vicar of Thorverton, and Prebendary of Exeter. 2 vols., 8vo., cloth, 1l. 4s. 6d.

The Volumes may be had separately, thus—Vol. I., 10s. 6d.; Vol. II., Part I., 6s.; Vol. II., Part II., 8s.

REV. T. LATHBURY.

A HISTORY OF THE BOOK OF COMMON PRAYER, AND OTHER AUTHORIZED BOOKS, from the Reformation; and an Attempt to ascertain how the Rubrics, Canons, and Customs of the Church have been understood and observed from the same time: with an Account of the State of Religion in England from 1640 to 1660. By the Rev. THOMAS LATHBURY, M.A., Author of "A History of the Convocation," &c. *Second Edition.* 8vo., 10s. 6d.

OXFORD LENTEN SERMONS.

PERSONAL RESPONSIBILITY OF MAN; AND THE PROPHETS OF THE LORD—THEIR MESSAGE TO THEIR OWN AGE AND TO OURS. Sermons preached during the SEASON OF LENT, 1868 and 1869, in Oxford, by the LORD BISHOP OF OXFORD; the DEAN OF ELY; H. L. MANSEL, D.D.; H. W. BURROWS, B.D.; the LORD ARCHBISHOP OF YORK; E. B. PUSEY, D.D.; A. POTT, B.D.; T. T. CARTER, M.A.; R. SCOTT, D.D.; W. J. IRONS, D.D.; the LORD BISHOP OF LINCOLN; J. R. WOODFORD, M.A.; H. P. LIDDON, M.A.; the LORD BISHOP OF DERBY; J. MOORHOUSE, M.A.; W. R. FREMANTLE, M.A.; and Ven. ARCHDEACON BICKERSTETH; with a Preface by the BISHOP OF OXFORD. 2 vols. 8vo., 12s. 6d.

REV. J. W. BURGON.

A PLAIN COMMENTARY ON THE FOUR HOLY GOSPELS, intended chiefly for Devotional Reading. 5 vols., Fcap. 8vo., cloth, £1 1s.

SHORT SERMONS (NINETY-ONE) FOR FAMILY READING: following the Course of the Christian Seasons. Second Series. By the Rev. JOHN W. BURGON, M.A., Fellow of Oriel, and Vicar of St. Mary-the-Virgin's. Now complete in Two Volumes. Fcap., cloth, 8s.

The First Series (Ninety) may also be had in Two Volumes, cloth, 8s.

REV. D. C. TIMINS.

FAMILY READINGS ON THE COLLECTS, EPISTLES, AND GOSPELS OF THE CHRISTIAN YEAR. By the Rev. DOUGLAS C. TIMINS, M.A., Oriel College, Oxford. Crown 8vo., cloth, 10s. 6d.

REV. DR. FRANCIS HESSEY.

CATECHETICAL LESSONS ON THE BOOK OF COMMON PRAYER. Illustrating the Prayer-book, from its Title-page to the end of the Collects, Epistles, and Gospels, and Designed to aid the Clergy in Public Catechising. By the Rev. Dr. FRANCIS HESSEY, Incumbent of St. Barnabas, Kensington, Author of "Catechetical Notes on the Parables and Miracles." Fcap. 8vo., cloth, 6s.

CATENA AUREA.

CATENA AUREA. A Commentary on the Four Gospels, collected out of the Works of the Fathers by S. THOMAS AQUINAS. Uniform with the Library of the Fathers. Re-issue. Complete in 6 vols., cloth. [*Nearly Ready.*

THOMAS A KEMPIS.

OF THE IMITATION OF CHRIST. FOUR BOOKS. By THOMAS A KEMPIS. A New Edition revised. On thick toned paper, with red border-lines, mediæval titles, ornamental initials, &c. Small 4to., ornamental cloth, 12s.

OF THE IMITATION OF CHRIST. Four Books. By THOMAS A KEMPIS. A new Edition, revised. Printed in red and black with red lines, on toned paper. Fcap., cloth antique, 4s.

TEXT-BOOKS FOR OXFORD EXAMINATIONS UNDER NEW THEOLOGICAL STATUTE.

THE DEFINITIONS OF THE CATHOLIC FAITH AND CANONS OF DISCIPLINE OF THE FIRST FOUR GENERAL COUNCILS OF THE UNIVERSAL CHURCH. In Greek and English. *2nd Edition.* Fcap. 8vo., cloth, 2s. 6d.

DE FIDE ET SYMBOLO: Documenta quædam nec non Aliquorum SS. Patrum Tractatus. Edidit CAROLUS A. HEURTLEY, S.T.P., Dom. Margaretæ Prælector, et Ædis Christi Canonicus. Fcap. 8vo., cloth, 4s. 6d.

S. AURELIUS AUGUSTINUS, Episcopus Hipponensis, de Catechizandis Rudibus, de Fide Rerum quæ non videntur, de Utilitate Credendi. In Usum Juniorum. Edidit C. MARRIOTT, S.T.B., Olim Coll. Oriel. Socius. *New Edition.* Fcap. 8vo., cloth, 3s. 6d.

ARCHDEACON CHURTON.

A MEMOIR OF THE LATE JOSHUA WATSON, ESQ. By the Venerable Archdeacon CHURTON. *A new and cheaper Edition, with Portrait.* Crown 8vo., cloth, 7s. 6d.

REV. H. W. BELLAIRS.

THE CHURCH AND THE SCHOOL; or, Hints on Clerical Life. By HENRY WALFORD BELLAIRS, M.A., one of Her Majesty's Inspectors of Schools. Crown 8vo., cloth, 5s.

REV. T. S. ACKLAND.

A SHORT SUMMARY OF THE EVIDENCES FOR THE BIBLE. By the Rev. T. S. ACKLAND, M.A., late Fellow of Clare Hall, Cambridge, Incumbent of Pollington-cum-Balne, Yorkshire. 24mo., cloth, 3s.

REV. C. A. HEURTLEY, D.D.

THE FORM OF SOUND WORDS: HELPS TOWARDS HOLDING IT FAST: Seven Sermons preached before the University of Oxford, on some Important Points of Faith and Practice. By CHARLES A. HEURTLEY, D.D., Margaret Professor of Divinity, and Canon of Christ Church. 8vo., cloth, 7s. 6d.

THE CATECHIST'S MANUAL.

THE CATECHIST'S MANUAL; with an Introduction by SAMUEL, LORD BISHOP OF OXFORD. *Fourth Thousand.* Crown 8vo., cloth, 5s.

REV. E. CHEERE.

THE CHURCH CATECHISM EXPLAINED. By the Rev. EDWARD CHEERE, M.A., Vicar of Little Drayton. Fcap., cloth, 2s. 6d.

SERMONS, &c.

PAROCHIAL SERMONS. By E. B. Pusey, D.D. From Advent to Whitsuntide. Vol. I. *Fifth Edition.* 8vo., cloth, 6s. Vol. II. *Fourth Edition.* 8vo., cloth, 6s.

NINE SERMONS PREACHED BEFORE THE UNIVERSITY OF OXFORD. By E. B. Pusey, D.D., and printed between 1843—1855. Now collected in one volume. 8vo., cloth, 7s. 6d.

PAROCHIAL SERMONS PREACHED AND PRINTED ON VARIOUS OCCASIONS. By E. B. PUSEY, D.D. Now collected in one volume. 8vo., cloth, 7s. 6d.

ILLUSTRATIONS OF FAITH. EIGHT PLAIN SERMONS, by a Writer in the "Tracts for the Christian Seasons" [the late Rev. EDWARD MONRO]:—Abel; Enoch; Noah; Abraham; Isaac, Jacob, and Joseph; Moses; The Walls of Jericho; Conclusions. Fcap. 8vo., cloth, 2s. 6d.

Uniform, and by the same Author,

PLAIN SERMONS ON THE BOOK OF COMMON PRAYER. Fcap. 8vo., cloth, 5s. HISTORICAL AND PRACTICAL SERMONS ON THE SUFFERINGS AND RESUR- RECTION OF OUR LORD. 2 vols., Fcap. 8vo., cloth, 10s. SERMONS ON NEW TESTAMENT CHARACTERS. Fcap. 8vo., 4s.

CHRISTIAN SEASONS.—Short and Plain Sermons for every Sunday and Holyday throughout the Year. Edited by the late Bishop of Grahamstown. 4 vols., Fcap. 8vo., cloth, 16s.

———————————— A Second Series of Sermons for the Christian Seasons. Uniform with the above. 4 vols., Fcap. 8vo., cloth, 16s.

ARMSTRONG'S PAROCHIAL SERMONS. Parochial Sermons, by JOHN ARMSTRONG, D.D., late Lord Bishop of Grahamstown. Fcap. 8vo., cl., 5s.

ARMSTRONG'S SERMONS FOR FASTS AND FESTIVALS. A new Edition. Fcap. 8vo., 5s.

SERMONS PREACHED BEFORE THE UNIVERSITY OF OXFORD, and in other places. By the late Rev. C. MARRIOTT, Fellow of Oriel College, Oxford. 12mo., cloth, 6s. Vol. II. 12mo., cloth, 7s. 6d.

SERMONS, CHIEFLY PRACTICAL. By the Rev. WILLIAM TOWNSEND HENHAM, M.A., of Christ's College, Cambridge. Post 8vo., cl., 5s.

SERMONS FOR THE HOLY SEASONS OF THE CHURCH. Advent to Trinity. By GEORGE HUNTINGTON, M.A., Rector of Tenby, and Domestic Chaplain to the Right Hon. the Earl of Crawford and Balcarres. *Second Edition.* Crown 8vo., cloth, 5s.

PAROCHIAL SERMONS, by the Rev. H. W. BURROWS, B.D., Perpetual Curate of Christ Church, St. Pancras. Second Series. Fcap. 5s.

SERMONS ADDRESSED TO THE CONGREGATION OF ST. MARY-LE-TOWER, IPSWICH. By the Rev. J. R. TURNOCK, M.A., Incumbent. Fcap. 8vo., cloth, 5s.

Works of the Standard English Divines,

PUBLISHED IN THE LIBRARY OF ANGLO-CATHOLIC THEOLOGY,

AT THE FOLLOWING PRICES IN CLOTH.

ANDREWES' (BP.) COMPLETE WORKS. 11 vols., 8vo., £3 7s.
THE SERMONS. (Separate.) 5 vols., £1 15s.

BEVERIDGE'S (BP.) COMPLETE WORKS. 12 vols., 8vo., £4 4s.
THE ENGLISH THEOLOGICAL WORKS. 10 vols., £3 10s.

BRAMHALL'S (ABP.) WORKS, WITH LIFE AND LETTERS, &c.
5 vols., 8vo., £1 15s. (Vol. 2 cannot be sold separately.)

BULL'S (BP.) HARMONY ON JUSTIFICATION. 2 vols., 8vo., 10s.

——————— DEFENCE OF THE NICENE CREED. 2 vols., 10s.

——————— JUDGMENT OF THE CATHOLIC CHURCH. 5s.

COSIN'S (BP.) WORKS COMPLETE. 5 vols., 8vo., £1 10s. (Vol. 1
cannot be sold separately.)

CRAKANTHORP'S DEFENSIO ECCLESIÆ ANGLICANÆ.
8vo., 7s.

FRANK'S SERMONS. 2 vols., 8vo., 10s.

FORBES' CONSIDERATIONES MODESTÆ. 2 vols., 8vo., 12s.

GUNNING'S PASCHAL, OR LENT FAST. 8vo., 6s.

HAMMOND'S PRACTICAL CATECHISM. 8vo., 5s.

——————— MISCELLANEOUS THEOLOGICAL WORKS. 5s.

——————— THIRTY-ONE SERMONS. 2 Parts. 10s.

HICKES'S TWO TREATISES ON THE CHRISTIAN PRIEST-
HOOD. 3 vols., 8vo., 15s.

JOHNSON'S (JOHN) THEOLOGICAL WORKS. 2 vols., 8vo., 10s.

——————— ENGLISH CANONS. 2 vols., 12s.

LAUD'S (ABP.) COMPLETE WORKS. 7 vols., (9 Parts,) 8vo.
£2 17s.

L'ESTRANGE'S ALLIANCE OF DIVINE OFFICES. 8vo., 6s.

MARSHALL'S PENITENTIAL DISCIPLINE. (This volume
cannot be sold separate from the complete set.)

NICHOLSON'S (BP.) EXPOSITION OF THE CATECHISM. (This
volume cannot be sold separate from the complete set.)

OVERALL'S (BP.) CONVOCATION-BOOK OF 1606. 8vo., 5s.

PEARSON'S (BP.) VINDICIÆ EPISTOLARUM S. IGNATII.
2 vols. 8vo., 10s.

THORNDIKE'S (HERBERT) THEOLOGICAL WORKS COM-
PLETE. 6 vols., (10 Parts,) 8vo., £2 10s.

WILSON'S (BP.) WORKS COMPLETE. With LIFE, by Rev.
J. KEBLE. 7 vols., (8 Parts,) 8vo., £3 3s.

A complete set, £25.

THE DAILY SERVICES OF THE CHURCH OF ENGLAND.
With an Introductory Preface by the LORD BISHOP OF OXFORD. Complete in
One Vol., Crown 8vo. The *Fifth Thousand.* Roan, 12s.; antique calf, red
edges, 16s.; best morocco, 18s.

DAILY STEPS TOWARDS HEAVEN; or, Practical Thoughts on
the Gospel History, and especially on the Life and Teaching of our Lord Jesus
Christ, for every day in the year, according to the Christian Seasons. With
Titles and Characters of Christ, and a Harmony of the Four Gospels. *Sixteenth
Edition.* 32mo., roan, 2s. 6d.; morocco, 4s. 6d.

———————— **LARGE-TYPE EDITION,** sq. cr. 8vo., cloth, 5s.

PRAYERS FOR MARRIED PERSONS. From Various Sources,
chiefly from the Ancient Liturgies. Selected and Edited by CHARLES WARD,
M.A., Rector of Maulden. *Second Edition,* revised and enlarged. 16mo.,
cloth, gilt edges, 4s. 6d.

THOUGHTS DURING SICKNESS. By the Author of " The Doc-
trine of the Cross," and " Devotions for the Sick Room." *Cheap Edit. preparing.*

BREVIATES FROM HOLY SCRIPTURE, arranged for use by the
Bed of Sickness. By the Rev. G. ARDEN, M.A., Rector of Winterborne-Came;
Domestic Chaplain to the Right Hon. the Earl of Devon. *2nd Ed.* Fcap. 8vo., 2s.

THE CURE OF SOULS. By the Same. Fcap. 8vo., 2s. 6d.

THE PASTOR IN HIS CLOSET; or, A Help to the Devotions
of the Clergy. By JOHN ARMSTRONG, D.D., late Lord Bishop of Grahamstown.
Third Edition. Fcap. 8vo., cloth, 2s.

OXFORD SERIES OF DEVOTIONAL WORKS. Fcap. 8vo.

The Imitation of Christ.
FOUR BOOKS. By Thomas à KEM-
PIS. Cloth, 4s.

Taylor's Holy Living.
THE RULE AND EXERCISES
OF HOLY LIVING. By BISHOP JEREMY
TAYLOR. Antique cloth, 4s.

Taylor's Holy Dying.
THE RULE AND EXERCISES
OF HOLY DYING. By BISHOP JEREMY
TAYLOR. Antique cloth, 4s.

Taylor's Golden Grove.
THE GOLDEN GROVE; a Choice
Manual, containing what is to be Believed,
Practised, and Desired, or Prayed for. By
BISHOP JEREMY TAYLOR. Printed uniform
with " Holy Living and Holy Dying." An-
tique cloth, 3s. 6d.

The 3 Volumes in antique cf. binding, £1 6s. 6d.

Sutton's Meditations.
GODLY MEDITATIONS UPON
THE MOST HOLY SACRAMENT OF THE
LORD'S SUPPER. By CHRISTOPHER SUT-
TON, D.D., late Prebend of Westminster.
A new Edition. Antique cloth, 5s.

Laud's Devotions.
THE PRIVATE DEVOTIONS of
DR. WILLIAM LAUD, Archbishop of Canter-
bury, and Martyr. Antique cloth, 5s.

Wilson's Sacra Privata.
THE PRIVATE MEDITATIONS,
DEVOTIONS, and PRAYERS of the Right
Rev. T. WILSON, D.D., Lord Bishop of Sodor
and Man. Now first printed entire. Cloth, 4s.

Andrewes' Devotions.
DEVOTIONS. By the Right Rev.
Father in God, LAUNCELOT ANDREWES.
Translated from the Greek and Latin, and
arranged anew. Antique cloth, 5s.

Spinckes' Devotions.
TRUE CHURCH OF ENGLAND
MAN'S COMPANION IN THE CLOSET;
or, a complete Manual of Private Devotions,
collected from the Writings of eminent Di-
vines of the Church of England. Floriated
borders, antique cloth, 4s.

Ancient Collects.
ANCIENT COLLECTS AND OTHER
PRAYERS. By WM. BRIGHT, D.D. *See p. 3.*

Devout Communicant.
THE DEVOUT COMMUNICANT,
exemplified in his Behaviour before, at, and
after the Sacrament of the Lord's Supper:
Practically suited to all the Parts of that
Solemn Ordinance. 7th Edition, revised.
Fcap. 8vo., toned paper, red lines, cloth, 4s.

ΕΙΚΩΝ ΒΑΣΙΛΙΚΗ.
THE PORTRAITURE OF HIS
SACRED MAJESTY KING CHARLES I.
in his Solitudes and Sufferings. Ant. cloth, 5s.

CORNISH BALLADS.

THE CORNISH BALLADS AND OTHER POEMS of the Rev. R. S. Hawker. Fcap. 8vo., cloth, 5s.

THE ENGLISH CAVALIERS.

LAYS OF THE ENGLISH CAVALIERS. By John J. Daniell, Perpetual Curate of Langley Fitzurse, Wilts. Small 4to., printed on toned paper, with Frontispiece and Vignette, ornamental cloth extra, gilt edges, 6s.

"THE CHRISTIAN YEAR."

THE CHRISTIAN YEAR. Thoughts in Verse for the Sundays and Holydays throughout the Year. *Foolscap Octavo Edition,*—Cloth, 7s. 6d.; morocco, 10s. 6d.; best morocco, 15s.; antique calf, 14s. *32mo. Edition,*—Cloth, 8s. 6d.; morocco, plain, 5s.; best morocco, 8s. 6d. *Cheap Edition,*—Cloth, 1s. 6d.; bound, 2s.

THE "LYRA INNOCENTIUM."

LYRA INNOCENTIUM. Thoughts in Verse on Christian Children. *Foolscap Octavo Edition,*—Cloth, 7s. 6d.; morocco, plain, 10s. 6d.; best morocco, 15s.; antique calf, 12s. *Cheap Edition,*—Cloth, 1s. 6d.; bound, 2s.

"THE CHILD'S CHRISTIAN YEAR."

THE CHILD'S CHRISTIAN YEAR. Hymns for every Sunday and Holyday throughout the Year. *Cheap Edition,* 18mo., cloth, 1s.

WORKS BY THE LATE ISAAC WILLIAMS.

THE CATHEDRAL. Foolscap 8vo., cloth, 7s. 6d.; 32mo., with Engravings, 4s. 6d.

THOUGHTS IN PAST YEARS. *The Sixth Edition,* with several new Poems, 32mo., cloth, 4s. 6d.

THE BAPTISTERY, OR THE WAY OF ETERNAL LIFE. By the Author of "The Cathedral." With Thirty-four Plates from Boetius a Bolswert. A new Edition, revised by the Author. 2 vols., Large Fcap. 8vo., cloth, 14s.

THE BAPTISTERY; or, The Way of Eternal Life. 32mo., cl., 3s. 6d.

THE CHRISTIAN SCHOLAR. Foolscap 8vo., 10s. 6d.; 32mo., cloth, 4s. 6d.

THE SEVEN DAYS; or, The Old and New Creation. *Second Edition,* Foolscap 8vo., 7s. 6d.

REV. W. V. HARCOURT.

WHAT IS TRUTH? A Poetical Dialogue on the Philosophy of Natural and Revealed Religion. By the Rev. William Vernon Harcourt, M.A., &c. Crown 8vo., cloth, 2s. 6d.

THE LITANY.

HYMNS ON THE LITANY. By A. C. Fcap. 8vo., on toned paper, cloth extra, 3s.

THE SECOND LESSONS.

MORNING THOUGHTS. By a Clergyman. Suggested by the Second Lessons for the Daily Morning Service throughout the year. 2 vols. Foolscap 8vo., cloth, 5s. each.

FLORUM SACRA. By the Rev. G. Hunt Smyttan. 16mo., 1s.

COXE'S CHRISTIAN BALLADS. Foolscap 8vo., cloth, 3s. Also selected Poems in a packet, sewed, 1s.

PROFESSOR GOLDWIN SMITH.

THE REORGANIZATION OF THE UNIVERSITY OF OXFORD.
By GOLDWIN SMITH. Post 8vo., limp cloth, 2s.

LECTURES ON THE STUDY OF HISTORY, DELIVERED IN
OXFORD, 1859—61. *Second Edition.* Crown 8vo., limp cloth, 3s. 6d.

IRISH HISTORY AND IRISH CHARACTER. *Second Edition.*
Post 8vo., 5s.

———————— Cheap Edition, Fcap. 8vo., sewed, 1s. 6d.

THE EMPIRE. A SERIES OF LETTERS PUBLISHED IN
"THE DAILY NEWS," 1862, 1863. Post 8vo., cloth, price 6s.

PROFESSOR BONAMY PRICE.

THE PRINCIPLES OF CURRENCY: Six Lectures delivered at
Oxford. By BONAMY PRICE, Professor of Political Economy in the University
of Oxford. With a Letter from M. MICHEL CHEVALIER, on the History of the
Treaty of Commerce with France. 8vo., cloth, 7s. 6d.

PROFESSOR DAUBENY.

MISCELLANIES: BEING A COLLECTION OF MEMOIRS and
ESSAYS ON SCIENTIFIC AND LITERARY SUBJECTS, published at
Various Times, by the late CHARLES DAUBENY, M.D., F.R.S., Professor of
Botany and of Rural Economy in the University of Oxford, &c. 2 vols., 8vo.,
cloth, 21s.

CLIMATE: An Inquiry into the Causes of its Differences, and into
its Influence on Vegetable Life. 8vo., cloth, price 4s.

LECTURES ON ROMAN HUSBANDRY: An Account of the
System of Agriculture, the Treatment of Domestic Animals, the Horticulture,
&c., pursued in Ancient Times. 8vo., cloth, 6s.

ESSAY ON THE TREES AND SHRUBS OF THE ANCIENTS:
Intended to be supplementary to Lectures on Roman Husbandry, already published. 8vo., limp cloth, lettered, 5s.

FUGITIVE POEMS, relating to Subjects connected with Natural
History and Physical Science, Archæology, &c. Selected by the late CHARLES
DAUBENY, &c. Fcap. 8vo., cl., 5s.

REV. L. BIGGE-WITHER.

A NEARLY LITERAL TRANSLATION OF HOMER'S ODYS-
SEY into ACCENTUATED DRAMATIC VERSE. By the Rev. LOVELACE
BIGGE-WITHER, M.A. Large fcap. 8vo., toned paper, cloth, 10s. 6d.

CHARLES ELTON.

THE TENURES OF KENT; or, A View of the Kentish Lands
which are not Gavelkind. Chiefly from Unpublished Records and MSS., with
many New Cases. By CHARLES ELTON, late Fellow of Queen's College,
Oxford; and of Lincoln's Inn, Barrister-at-Law. Royal 8vo., cloth, 1l. 6s.

NORWAY: THE ROAD AND THE FELL. By CHARLES ELTON,
late Fellow of Queen's College, Oxford. Post 8vo., cloth, price 7s. 6d.

HENRICUS DENISON.

GULIELMI SHAKSPERII JULIUS CÆSAR. Latine reddidit
HENRICUS DENISON, Col. Om. An. apud Oxon. Olim Socius. *Second Edition.*
8vo., with red border lines, cloth, 6s.

THE PRAYER-BOOK CALENDAR.

THE CALENDAR OF THE PRAYER-BOOK ILLUSTRATED.
(Comprising the first portion of the "Calendar of the Anglican Church," with additional Illustrations, &c.) With Two Hundred Engravings from Medieval Works of Art. *Sixth Thousand.* Fcap. 8vo., cloth, 6s.

THE LATE CHARLES WINSTON.

AN INQUIRY INTO THE DIFFERENCE OF STYLE OBSERV-
ABLE IN ANCIENT GLASS PAINTINGS, especially in England, with Hints on Glass Painting, by the late CHARLES WINSTON. With Corrections and Additions by the Author. 2 vols., Medium 8vo., cloth, £1 11s. 6d.

REV. JOHN PUCKLE.

THE CHURCH AND FORTRESS OF DOVER CASTLE. By
the Rev. JOHN PUCKLE, M.A., Vicar of St. Mary's, Dover; Rural Dean. With Illustrations from the Author's Drawings. Medium 8vo., cloth, 7s. 6d.

G. G. SCOTT, F.S.A.

GLEANINGS FROM WESTMINSTER ABBEY. By GEORGE
GILBERT SCOTT, R.A., F.S.A. With Appendices supplying Further Particulars, and completing the History of the Abbey Buildings, by Several Writers. *Second Edition,* enlarged, containing many new Illustrations by O. Jewitt and others. Medium 8vo., 15s.

REV. SAMUEL LYSONS, F.S.A.

OUR BRITISH ANCESTORS: WHO AND WHAT WERE
THEY? An Inquiry serving to elucidate the Traditional History of the Early Britons by means of recent Excavations, Etymology, Remnants of Religious Worship, Inscriptions, Craniology, and Fragmentary Collateral History. By the Rev. SAMUEL LYSONS, M.A., F.S.A., Rector of Rodmarton, and Perpetual Curate of St. Luke's, Gloucester. Post 8vo., cloth, 12s.

M. VIOLLET-LE-DUC.

THE MILITARY ARCHITECTURE OF THE MIDDLE AGES,
Translated from the French of M. VIOLLET-LE-DUC. By M. MACDERMOTT, Esq., Architect. With the 151 original French Engravings. Medium 8vo., cloth, £1 1s.

JOHN HEWITT.

ANCIENT ARMOUR AND WEAPONS IN EUROPE. By JOHN
HEWITT, Member of the Archæological Institute of Great Britain. Vols. II. and III., comprising the Period from the Fourteenth to the Seventeenth Century, completing the work, 1l. 12s. Also Vol. I., from the Iron Period of the Northern Nations to the end of the Thirteenth Century, 18s. The work complete, 3 vols., 8vo., 2l. 10s.

REV. PROFESSOR STUBBS.

THE TRACT "DE INVENTIONE SANCTÆ CRUCIS NOSTRÆ
IN MONTE ACUTO ET DE DUCTIONE EJUSDEM APUD WALT-HAM," now first printed from the Manuscript in the British Museum, with Introduction and Notes by WILLIAM STUBBS, M.A., Vicar of Navestock, late Fellow of Trinity College, Oxford. Royal 8vo., uniform with the Works issued by the Master of the Rolls, (only 100 copies printed,) price 5s.; Demy 8vo., 3s. 6d.

HENRY GODWIN, F.S.A.

THE ARCHÆOLOGIST'S HANDBOOK. By HENRY GODWIN, F.S.A.
This work contains a summary of the materials which are available for the investigation of the Monuments of this country, arranged chiefly under their several successive periods, from the earliest times to the fifteenth century,—together with Tables of Dates, Kings, &c., Lists of Coins, Cathedrals, Castles, Monasteries, &c. Crown 8vo., cloth, 7s. 6d.

JOHN HENRY PARKER, F.S.A., HON. M.A. OXON.

THE EARLY CHRISTIAN AND MEDIÆVAL ANTIQUITIES
OF ROME. By John Henry Parker, F.S.A., Hon. M.A. Oxon. Medium
8vo. Illustrated by Woodcuts.   [*In the Press.*

AN INTRODUCTION TO THE STUDY OF GOTHIC ARCHI-
TECTURE. By John Henry Parker, F.S.A., Hon. M.A. Oxon. *Third
Edition*, Revised and Enlarged, with 160 Illustrations, and a Glossarial Index.
Fcap. 8vo., cloth lettered, 5s.

A CONCISE GLOSSARY OF TERMS USED IN GRECIAN,
ROMAN, ITALIAN, AND GOTHIC ARCHITECTURE. By John
Henry Parker, F.S.A., Hon. M.A. Oxon. A New Edition, revised. Fcap.
8vo., with 470 Illustrations, in ornamental cloth, 7s. 6d.

The "Abridgment of the Glossary of Architecture" met with a rapid sale some years ago,
since which time it has remained out of print. It is now reprinted with very numerous additions and alterations.

THE ARCHITECTURAL ANTIQUITIES OF THE CITY OF
WELLS. By John Henry Parker, F.S.A., Hon. M.A. Oxon., Honorary
Member of the Somerset Archæological Society, &c. Illustrated by Plans and
Views. Medium 8vo., cloth, 5s.

ILLUSTRATIONS OF ARCHITECTURAL ANTIQUITIES.

WELLS: 32 Photographs, Folio size, in portfolio, price 3*l.* 3s.; or separately,
2s. 6d. each.
     Also 16 Photographs, in 8vo., reduced from the above, in a case, price 15s.;
     or separately, 1s. each.
GLASTONBURY ABBEY: 9 Photographs, Folio size, in portfolio, price 1*l.*; or separately, 2s. 6d. each.
DORSETSHIRE: 23 Photographs, Folio size, in portfolio, price 4*l.* 4s.; or separately,
2s. 6d. each.

AN ATTEMPT TO DISCRIMINATE THE STYLES OF AR-
CHITECTURE IN ENGLAND, FROM THE CONQUEST TO THE
REFORMATION: WITH A SKETCH OF THE GRECIAN AND
ROMAN ORDERS. By the late Thomas Rickman, F.S.A. *Sixth Edition*,
with considerable Additions, chiefly Historical, by John Henry Parker, F.S.A.,
Hon. M.A. Oxon., and numerous Illustrations by O. Jewitt. 8vo., cloth, 1*l.* 1s.

SOME ACCOUNT OF DOMESTIC ARCHITECTURE IN ENG-
LAND, from Richard II. to Henry VIII. (or the Perpendicular Style). With
Numerous Illustrations of Existing Remains from Original Drawings. By the
Editor of "The Glossary of Architecture." In 2 vols., 8vo., 1*l.* 10s.

Also,

FROM EDWARD I. TO RICHARD II. (the Edwardian Period, or the
Decorated Style). 8vo., 21s.

THE MEDIÆVAL ARCHITECTURE OF CHESTER. By John
Henry Parker, F.S.A., Hon. M.A. Oxon. With an Historical Introduction
by the Rev. Francis Grosvenor. Illustrated by Engravings by J. H. Le
Keux, O. Jewitt, &c. 8vo., cloth, 5s.

REV. L. M. HUMBERT, M.A.

MEMORIALS OF THE HOSPITAL OF ST. CROSS AND ALMS-
HOUSE OF NOBLE POVERTY. By the Rev. L. M. Humbert, M.A.,
Master of St. Cross. Illustrated with Thirteen Photographs, by W. Savage,
and numerous Woodcuts. 4to., cloth extra, gilt edges, 15s.; morocco elegant, 30s.

J. T. BLIGHT, F.S.A.

THE CROMLECHS OF CORNWALL: with some Account of other
Prehistoric Sepulchral Monuments, and Articles found in connection with them,
in the same County. By J. T. Blight, F.S.A. Medium 8vo., with numerous
Illustrations.   [*In the Press.*

THE NEW SCHOOL-HISTORY OF ENGLAND, from Early Writers and the National Records. By the Author of "The Annals of England." Crown 8vo., with Four Maps, limp cloth, 5s.

ANNALS OF ENGLAND. An Epitome of English History. From Cotemporary Writers, the Rolls of Parliament, and other Public Records. 3 vols. Fcap. 8vo., with Illustrations, cloth, 15s. *Recommended by the Examiners in the School of Modern History at Oxford.*

Vol. I. From the Roman Era to the Death of Richard II. Cloth, 5s.

Vol. II. From the Accession of the House of Lancaster to Charles I. Cloth, 5s.

Vol. III. From the Commonwealth to the Death of Queen Anne. Cloth, 5s.

JELF'S GREEK GRAMMAR.—A Grammar of the Greek Language, chiefly from the text of Raphael Kühner. By Wm. Edw. Jelf, B.D., late Student and Censor of Ch. Ch. *Fourth Edition, with Additions and Corrections.* 2 vols. 8vo., 1l. 10s.

This Grammar is in general use at Oxford, Cambridge, Dublin, and Durham; at Eton, King's College, London, and most other public schools.

MADVIG'S LATIN GRAMMAR. A Latin Grammar for the Use of Schools. By Professor Madvig, with additions by the Author. Translated by the Rev. G. Woods, M.A. Uniform with Jelf's "Greek Grammar." *New Edition.* 8vo., cloth, 12s.

Competent authorities pronounce this work to be the very best Latin Grammar yet published in England. This new Edition contains an Index to the Authors quoted.

THE ETHICS OF ARISTOTLE. With Notes by the Rev. W. E. Jelf, B.D., Author of "A Greek Grammar," &c. 8vo., cloth, 12s.

The Text separately, 5s. The Notes separately, 7s. 6d.

LAWS OF THE GREEK ACCENTS. By John Griffiths, M.A. *New Edition.* 16mo. Price Sixpence. *(Uniform with Oxford Pocket Classics.)*

TWELVE RUDIMENTARY RULES FOR LATIN PROSE COM- POSITION: with Examples and Exercises, for the use of Beginners. By the Rev. Edward Moore, D.D., Principal of St. Edmund Hall, Oxford, and late Fellow and Tutor of Queen's College. 16mo., 6d. *(Uniform with Oxford Pocket Classics.)*

THUCYDIDES, with Notes, chiefly Historical and Geographical. By the late T. Arnold, D.D. With Indices by the Rev. R. P. G. Tiddeman. *Sixth Edition.* 3 vols., 8vo., cloth lettered, £1 16s.

ERASMI COLLOQUIA SELECTA: Arranged for Translation and Re-translation; adapted for the Use of Boys who have begun the Latin Syntax. By Edward C. Lowe, D.D., Head Master of S. John's Middle School, Hurst-pierpoint. Fcap. 8vo., strong binding, 3s.

PORTA LATINA: A Selection from Latin Authors, for Translation and Re-Translation; arranged in a Progressive Course, as an Introduction to the Latin Tongue. By Edward C. Lowe, D.D., Head Master of Hurstpierpoint School; Editor of Erasmus' "Colloquies," &c. Fcap. 8vo., strongly bound, 3s.

TRILINEAR CO-ORDINATES. With Examples. Intended chiefly for the Use of Junior Students. By C. J. C. Price, M.A., Fellow and Mathematical Lecturer of Exeter College, Oxford. Post 8vo., cloth, 8s.

NOTES ON THE GEOMETRY OF THE PLANE TRIANGLE. By John Griffiths, M.A., Mathematical Lecturer of Jesus College, Oxford. Crown 8vo., cloth, 4s.

A SERIES OF GREEK AND LATIN CLASSICS
FOR THE USE OF SCHOOLS.

GREEK POETS.

	Cloth. *s. d.*		Cloth. *s. d.*
Æschylus	. 3 0	Sophocles . . .	. 3 0
Aristophanes. 2 vols. .	. 6 0	Homeri Ilias : :	. 3 6
Euripides. 3 vols. .	. 6 6	———— Odyssea . .	. 3 0
———— Tragœdiæ Sex	. 3 6		

GREEK PROSE WRITERS.

	s. d.		*s. d.*
Aristotelis Ethica .	. 2 0	Thucydides. 2 vols. .	. 5 0
Demosthenes de Corona, et } Æschines in Ctesiphontem }	2 0	Xenophontis Memorabilia	. 1 4
		———————— Anabasis .	. 2 0
Herodotus. 2 vols. .	. 6 0		

LATIN POETS.

	s. d.		*s. d.*
Horatius . . .	. 2 0	Lucretius . . .	. 2 0
Juvenalis et Persius .	. 1 6	Phædrus . . .	. 1 4
Lucanus	. 2 6	Virgilius . . .	. 2 6

LATIN PROSE WRITERS.

			s. d.
Cæsaris Commentarii, cum Sup- plementisAuliHirtii et aliorum	2 6	Ciceronis Orationes Selectæ, *in the Press.*	
———— Commentarii de Bello Gallico . . .	1 6	Cornelius Nepos . .	. 1 4
		Livius. 4 vols. . .	. 6 0
Cicero De Officiis, de Senectute, et de Amicitia . .	2 0	Sallustius . . .	. 2 0
Ciceronis Tusc. Disp. Lib. V.	2 0	Tacitus. 2 vols. . .	. 5 0

TEXTS WITH SHORT NOTES.

UNIFORM WITH THE SERIES OF "OXFORD POCKET CLASSICS."

GREEK WRITERS. TEXTS AND NOTES.
SOPHOCLES.

	s. d.		*s. d.*
Ajax (*Text and Notes*) .	. 1 0	Antigone (*Text and Notes*)	· 1 0
Electra „ .	. 1 0	Philoctetes „ . .	. 1 0
Œdipus Rex „ .	. 1 0	Trachiniæ „ . .	. 1 0
Œdipus Coloneus „	. 1 0		

The Notes only, in one vol., cloth, 3*s.*

ÆSCHYLUS.

	s. d.		*s. d.*
Persæ (*Text and Notes*) .	. 1 0	Choephoræ (*Text and Notes*) .	1 0
Prometheus Vinctus „	. 1 0	Eumenides „ .	. 1 6
Septem Contra Thebas „	. 1 0	Supplices „ .	. 1 0
Agamemnon „	. 1 0		

.The Notes only, in one vol., cloth, 3s. 6d.

EURIPIDES.

	s. d.		s. d.
Hecuba (*Text and Notes*)	. 1 0	Phœnissæ (*Text and Notes*) .	1 0
Medea " .	. 1 0	Alcestis " .	1 0
Orestes " .	. 1 0	The above Notes only, in one vol., cloth, 3s.	
Hippolytus " .	. 1 0	Bacchæ " .	1 0

ARISTOPHANES.

The Knights (*Text and Notes*)	1 0	The Birds (*Texts and Notes*) .	1 6
Acharnians "	1 0	The Frogs, *in preparation.*	

HOMERUS . . . . . . Ilias, Lib. i.—vi. (*Text and Notes*) . 2 0

DEMOSTHENES.

De Corona (*Text and Notes*) . 2 0 | Olynthiac Orations . . 1 0
Philippic Orations, *in the Press.*

ÆSCHINES . . . . . . In Ctesiphontem (*Text and Notes*) . 2 0

LATIN WRITERS. TEXTS AND NOTES.

VIRGILIUS.

Bucolica (*Text and Notes*)	. 1 0	Æneidos, Lib. i.—iii. (*Text*	
Georgica "	. 2 0	*and Notes*) . .	. 1 0

HORATIUS.

Carmina, &c. (*Text and Notes*)	2 0	Epistolæ et Ars Poetica (*Texts*	
Satiræ "	. 1 0	*and Notes*) . .	. 1 0

The Notes only, in one vol., cloth, 2s.

PHÆDRUS . . . Fabulæ (*Text and Notes*) 1 0

LIVIUS . . . . Lib. xxi.—xxiv. (*Text and Notes*) sewed, 4s.; cloth, 4 6

SALLUSTIUS.

Jugurtha (*Text and Notes*) . 1 6 | Catilina (*Text and Notes*) . 1 0

M. T. CICERO.

Pro Milone (*Text and Notes*) .	1 0	In Q. Cæcilium — Divinatio	
In Catilinam "	. 1 0	(*Text and Notes*) . .	. 1 0
Pro Lege Manilia, et Pro		In Verrem Actio Prima .	. 1 0
Archia " .	. 1 0	Epistolæ Selectæ. Pars I. .	1 6
De Senectute et De Amici-		Orationes Philippicæ, I., II.	1 6
tia	. 1 0		

CÆSAR . . . . Lib. i.—iii. (*Text and Notes*) . . . 1 0
CORNELIUS NEPOS. Lives (*Text and Notes*) . . . 1 6
TACITUS. ANNALS, *in the Press.*

Other portions of several of the above-named Authors are in preparation.

POETARUM SCENICORUM GRÆCORUM, Æschyli, Sophoclis, Euripidis, et Aristophanis, Fabulæ, Superstites, et Perditarum Fragmenta. Ex recognitione GUIL. DINDORFII. Editio Quinta. Royal 8vo., cloth, 21s.

Uniform with the Oxford Pocket Classics.

THE LIVES OF THE MOST EMINENT ENGLISH POETS; WITH CRITICAL OBSERVATIONS ON THEIR WORKS. By Samuel Johnson. 3 vols., 24mo., cloth, 3s. 6d. each.

CHOICE EXTRACTS FROM MODERN FRENCH AUTHORS, for the use of Schools. [*In the Press.*

* Price 4s.
# THE OXFORD UNIVERSITY CALENDAR 1870. Corrected to the end of Michaelmas Term, 1869.   [*In February.*

12mo., cloth, price 5s.; black roan, 5s. 6d.

THE OXFORD TEN-YEAR BOOK: A Volume Supplementary to the "Oxford University Calendar." This Volume has an Index which shews at once all the academical honours and offices of every person comprised in the lists, which date from the earliest times in the history of the University to the present. The first of these decennial volumes is made up to the end of the year 1860; the second will be issued after the end of 1870. The CALENDAR itself will be published annually as before, and will contain all the Class Lists, and all the names of Officers, Professors, and others, accruing since the date of the preceding TEN-YEAR BOOK.

THE OXFORD UNIVERSITY EXAMINATION PAPERS, printed directly from the Examiners' Copies. From 1863 to 1869. Most of the back Examination Papers may still be obtained, a few only being out of print.

EXAMINATION PAPERS IN LAW AND MODERN HISTORY. From 1863 to 1868. In One Volume, cloth, 7s. 6d.

——— IN THE SCHOOL OF NATURAL SCIENCE. From 1863 to 1868. 7s. 6d.

——— IN DISCIPLINIS MATHEMATICIS. From 1863 to 1868. 7s. 6d.

——— IN SCIENTIIS MATHEMATICIS ET PHYSICIS. From 1863 to 1868. 7s. 6d.

FOR THE ACADEMICAL YEAR ENDING JULY, 1869.

Copies of each may be had separately, as follows :—

Michaelmas, 1868.	s.	d.	Hilary, 1869.	s.	d.
No.			No.		
91. Responsions	0	6	98. Responsions	0	6
92. 1st Public, Lit. Græc. et Lat.	1	0	*Trinity, 1869.*		
95. 1st Public, Disc. Math.	1	0	99. Responsions	0	6
94. 2nd Public, Nat. Science	1	0	102. 1st Public, Lit. Græc. et Lat.	1	0
93. 2nd Public, Law and Hist.	1	0	104. 1st Public, Disc. Math.	1	0
96. 2nd Public, Math. et Phys.	1	0	100. 2nd Public, Lit. Hum.	1	0
97. 2nd Public, Lit. Hum.	1	0	101. 2nd Public, Law and Hist.	1	0
			103. 2nd Public, Nat. Science	1	0
			105. 2nd Public, Math. et Phys.	1	0

These are printed directly from the official copies used by the Examiners in the Schools.

PASS AND CLASS: An Oxford Guide-Book through the Courses of *Literæ Humaniores,* Mathematics, Natural Science, and Law and Modern History. By MONTAGU BURROWS, Chichele Professor of Modern History. *Third Edition.* Revised and Enlarged; with Appendices on the Indian Civil Service, the Diplomatic Service, and the Local Examinations. Fcap. 8vo., cloth, price 5s.

www.ingramcontent.com/pod-product-compliance
Lightning Source LLC
Chambersburg PA
CBHW031121020726
47495CB00007B/2291